IN THE CLEFT

JOY COMES IN THE MOURNING

A STORY OF HOPE AFTER TRAGEDY

DANA GOODMAN

PRESS

In the Cleft: Joy Comes In the Mourning
A Story of Hope After Tragedy
by Dana Goodman

Printed in the United States of America

ISBN 9781498408745

www.xulonpress.com

I dedicate this book to my hero and son, Zach Laird, who lived fully, richly, and selflessly. He laughed when there was nothing to laugh about and persevered when everyone else I know would have given up. Zach is my teacher, leading me toward greater faith and love. Zach points me to Christ in the way he loved, forgave, and saw the best in all people. I miss you forever, Zach.

Zach at Sunset Beach in Oahu
during his Make-A-Wish Trip

SPECIAL THANKS TO MY EDITORS

What an incredible journey this book has been. With countless cases of writer's block and many tearful, sleepless nights, my dream of writing my family's story is finally a reality. I could not have done it without my friend and editor, Bonnie Bylsma, who worked tirelessly with me through the whole process. When I thought I could not write one more word, Bonnie lovingly, yet persistently, stretched me to go a little bit further. I also want to thank Susan Duncan, Karen Hayes and Dina Chase for helping me add the finishing touches. All of you have been a blessing.

TABLE OF CONTENTS

He hideth my soul in the cleft of the rock,
That shadows a dry, thirsty land;
He hideth my life with the depths of his love,
And covers me there with his hand.

—Fanny Crosby

FOREWORD

This is a story of my family's journey through the valley of sorrows. Here, you will find pain and joy mingling together, dancing side by side. While writing, I had to practice being vulnerable again and again, because I continually found myself resisting transparency. Opening the doors of my heart to visit rooms that had been bolted shut felt unbearable at times. Drawing deep on my courage, I began to pry open unspoken cries, aches, longings and disappointments. The layers of grief were almost impossible to put into words, and when I did find language, it felt inadequate to describe the depth and poignancy of my journey through the valley. I have chosen not to gloss over my suffering in hopes that my pain will give voice to others travelling through their own valleys.

Writing this story has been like trying to patch together pieces of a quilt, some pieces beautiful and others tattered and torn. Missing pieces required me to revisit painful memories, rummaging through and searching for meaning. Unfolding layers of trauma was like ripping a bandage off a partially healed wound. Aggravated, the wound bled and hurt as though it had just happened. I felt re-traumatized. Rogue waves of grief left me surrounded by wadded tissue. But Jesus wept with me. Enfolded in his love, I sensed his gentle invitation to lay the painful memories of my life out on the table to be sifted through with him.

During our passage through the valley, God sheltered me under the shadow of his wings. He carved out a place for he and I to go so he could comfort my grieving soul. I felt his nurturing, protective presence sustaining me during my darkest times. In the Bible, Moses has an encounter with God and God promises he "will put [Moses] in a cleft in the rock and cover [him] with [his] hand." (Exodus 33:22) The hands that covered Moses are the same ones that cradle us when we are in overwhelming situations. Clefts are places of refuge. Birds hide in them to get away from dangerous predators and to escape the harsh winter seasons. Similarly, the cleft was a place I could hide during long winter seasons of emotional pain.

Moments in the cleft were often fleeting, short-lived respites, but those moments gave me enough strength to continue through the long stretches of suffering and pain. When I would tuck into God's resting place, it felt as though an umbilical cord attached the two of us together. He poured his sustenance into me so I could endure the long haul. His voice hushed my fear. Throughout my journey, I sensed Jesus contending for me, and though I did not always experience his presence, I held onto the promise that a new day would come. In the cleft he made me brave, so I could get through one more day. His tears mixed with my tears. I did not have to explain myself; he knew. Just when I would start to believe his promises of love, joy and peace were a sham, God would draw me back into the cleft where heaven's rain would wash away the effects of trauma enough so I could see hints of his greater redemptive work. Joy in mourning is a knowing that goes beyond feelings. Feelings can be fickle, changing from one moment to the next. But true, deeper joy anchors itself to the promises of Christ. His promises never change no matter what we are feeling or what we are going through. Whatever road of suffering we have to walk in this life, all will be well in the end. Whatever darkness I have to endure, I will go through it with Jesus.

Braving the dark places has taken my healing to a deeper level. In some ways, I still feel my life lies in shattered ruins with mounds of broken dreams smoldering before me; yet, in other ways, I feel more complete. I am more in tune with the ache of the world. My heart hurts for what hurts God's heart. Parts of me will never be all right again. I will always be different than I was before the tragedies. But parts of me have never felt more whole and connected with the things of heaven. Pain has compelled me to look at life differently. It has a way of setting priorities in the right order. On this side of heaven, I will always ache for what I have no more, but I will never be without hope. In the gap between now and heaven, Jesus tethers me to himself, giving me what I need to walk out this earthly journey.

What you have before you is a book of snapshots, a quilt of God's love story as he helped my family and I see that joy does come in the mourning. This is a story of tragedy and hope. I give you all God taught me in the night season. I invite you on my journey to laugh, grieve, worship, ponder, and celebrate with me. May each of you receive rich blessings from the throne room of heaven.

Love to all,
Dana

You saw my bones being formed as I took shape in my mother's body. When I was put together there, you saw my body as it was formed. All the days planned for me were written in your book before I was one day old.

—Psalm 139:15-16 (NCV)

CHAPTER 1

WHO'S WHO

From sea to shining sea, tempests are to be expected in our
weather patterns and in our lives.

—Patsy Clairmont

Our family is different than many families. Pain has defined so much
of our lives. Often, sadness greeted us in the morning and then
bid us goodnight in the evening. Cancer, in its serrated ugliness, stole
away my husband, my son and my mother-in-law, all within a period of
eight years. These losses have left a void in my heart that is galaxy-wide.
Grief took me to uncharted places I never imagined I would have to
travel. Often lost amidst ocean swells of emotions, I had no idea how to
manoeuvre through the darkness. Like a violent twister, death intruded
on our family and snatched away our dreams and hopes. After one storm
ravaged through our lives, we would have a short reprieve, only to have
another one strike, fiercer than the one before.

My earliest remembrance of cancer's ruthlessness goes back to when I was six years old. After a fun day of skiing at Hudson Bay Mountain in Smithers, British Columbia, our family huddled together in our tiny camper playing our favourite card game, Crazy Eights. My Dad ski patrolled, so he always carried his Walkie Talkie. Our Crazy Eight game was interrupted when he was paged to come to the ski patrol hut to take a phone call. The sadness in my Dad's eyes when he returned to the camper frightened me, and his news scared me even more: "Grandma has cancer." At that time, I had never heard about cancer, but dread welled in my heart because I knew something awful had happened.

My Grandma Smith was my favourite. She understood me like no other. Her eyes danced with joy and she filled a room with laughter and kindness. I always wanted to be near her because I felt protected and cherished. Not used to big cities, my sister Margie and I often felt scared at night when we had sleepovers at her home in Vancouver. We would lie awake in the dark, staring at the open closet, imagining the buttons on the clothing were eyes staring back at us. Finally, not able to handle our fear any longer, we would bolt to my grandma's room, knowing she would snuggle us in her big bed and soothe away our worries. We never felt like an inconvenience to her. When I walked beside her, I held my head high because she made me feel like nothing in the world was as great as me. One evening, after sightseeing all day in Vancouver, she took me into a department store. I fell in love with a dress on one of the mannequins. All I had to do was look at it, and she said, "Darling, I think that dress would look beautiful on you." The next thing I knew, I was all dressed up, with curls in my hair having a photo shoot in my favourite dress. Along with making Margie and I feel uniquely special, my grandma delighted us with special surprises. She would tuck us into bed, for example, and then suddenly get a mischievous look on her face and say, "Hey, who wants to go to White Spot?" With that, we would pile into her yellow car in our pajamas and go for Pirate Paks. My grandma was inwardly beautiful, but she was also physically stunning. She wore bright red nail polish and had charm bracelets that jingled whenever she became overly animated. I wanted nothing more than to grow up to be just like her. I would imitate her, painting my nails and clinking my charm bracelet just like she did. Her favourite colour was yellow, so mine was too.

During the time my grandma was sick, I remember being shocked when I walked into her room. My beautiful grandma looked nothing as I remembered her. Cancer had ravished her body. Her sparkly eyes now looked dull and tired. Her sickness scared me, yet her warm kind voice put me at ease. She tenderly drew me close and, as always, she had a gift for me. She gave me a pointer stick she had used while teaching at Langara College in Vancouver. At the time, I did not understand the significance of her gift, but now I understand she was speaking into my destiny. All these years later, I can hear her saying, "Darling, you have something important to share with the world. Teach them what is in your heart." Even though I was painfully shy at the time, she saw something greater in me than I would ever see in myself. Her death left a hole in my heart. I often wonder how my life would have been different had she lived and mentored me throughout my growing up years.

For most of my early childhood, I lived in Tweedsmuir Provincial Park in the west Chilcotin area of BC. We lived in a small wooden cabin, isolated from most of the world. Margie and I had limitless time to explore the natural world around us. We would put on our mosquito nets first thing in the morning and go outside to play for hours. One of our favourite things to do was find birch bark and use it as paper to colour on. We would paint pet rocks and play with them for hours in the dirt. Our lives were not structured or organized with play dates, preschool, sports events or clubs. We just went outside and played with rocks, sticks and other natural objects. Our lives were simple and uncomplicated. My dad was the park ranger, so he would take my sister and I with him on multi-day mountainous adventures, mostly in the Rainbow Mountain

Range on the western edge of the Chilcotin Plateau. Dad educated us at a young age all about the backcountry. He taught us the names of flowers, birds, constellations and mountain ranges. When we went hiking, he would often pause and tell us to close our eyes and listen. "Do you hear all the sounds?" he would ask. We would go a little bit farther and he would stop again, this time asking us to open our eyes and notice details in nature. He would pick out a spot and then have us tell him all we saw in that tiny area. We would get down on our knees and find critters, details in flowers, tiny seeds, and other small bits of beauty. "There is always something to see if you take the time to look," he would say. He passed on his love of nature to us. To this day, the outdoors feels like home to me.

Perhaps the simplicity of those early years is what made coping with the world so difficult for me during my school years. I could not adjust to chaos around me. From a young age, I wrestled with my sensitive heart. For as long as I can remember, I have been overly conscientious and turned inward to deeper things beyond my physical years. Perceptive to the emotional environment around me, I felt easily overwhelmed and burdened for others. I carried other people's pain as though it was my own, making it excruciatingly difficult to cope with my own day-to-day life. Not surprisingly, I was prone to anxiety and depression. I did not know how to navigate life as one who felt so intensely. During my grade five year, all students in my class received a Gideon Bible. At this time, I began to ponder spiritual things. I started reading the Old Testament and perceived God as punitive and void of love. I became terrified of him, thinking he was angry and vindictive. I started making lists of all I needed to do so I would be acceptable to him. Fear immobilized me. The darkness became so thick that year, I was unable to attend school for a month. My teachers were concerned because I cried all of the time. Childhood depression became my reality.

Slowly, I forced my way out of the darkness, but with a numb heart. I learned to cope with the barrage of emotions by dissociating from my tenderness. Life seemed easier that way and I felt less vulnerable. I still had empathy for others, but not to the extent I did in my earlier years. I decided to put any concept of God on the shelf. My experience with him had been too painful. From time to time, I would occasionally feel the darkness closing in, but full-blown depression did not rear its head again until my first year at University College of the Cariboo, now Thompson Rivers University. Life at university paralyzed me because it felt so intimidating. In addition to my trouble coping with school, my parents' separation during that time sent me into a tailspin. Life seemed to have so many twists and turns that were unpredictable and heart wrenching. My world seemed unstable and unsafe. I felt this pain deeply.

After graduating with my Bachelor of Arts in English Literature in 1994, I began to emerge from my deep sadness. I seemed to come into my own sense of self. I became more confident, more joyful and more passionate about life. Perfection no longer seemed so important. I felt like I had a new lease on life and took it more lightly. At the end of August 1995, I moved to Vancouver to take a one-year intensive teaching degree at the University of British Columbia. During my first year, I connected with a friend I had gone to high school with in Kamloops, Jason Laird. When I had known him in high school, he had been kind and gentle, yet furiously competitive, making him both lovable and confident. Throughout his schooling, he was frequently honoured with citizenship awards for his kindness toward others. He never really fit into a particular group or mould. When he was captain of the football team, his teammates teased him relentlessly for having to leave practice early to go to flute lessons. When we reconnected at a UBC forestry party in 1996, we instantly felt attracted to each other. Both of us were sensitive, yet adventurous. We had similar dreams and passions. Jay's humility stood out to me. He seemed more interested in others' stories than boasting about his own. Within a few months, we linked up again at Lou's Bar and Grill on Broadway in Vancouver and began dating.

On one of our first dates, Jay thought it would be adventurous and romantic to kayak down Seymour River in Vancouver. Rain over the past weeks had left the river in flood stage, which should have been the first indication to me that his plan had disaster written all over it. The raging water and my inept paddling were a terrible combination. "Whatever you do, don't go down the middle of the river," Jay warned before we paddled off from shore. "Just ferry to the other side." For a seasoned paddler, his plan made perfect sense, but with my talent, I would have had more success walking on water. Needless to say, I got sucked down the middle of the river. Jay could not find an eddy to park his boat and help me. I floundered, panic stricken, trying to get my uncooperative kayak across the river. Of course, I did not know how to do a roll, so when I flipped, I had to pull off the spray cover and push my way out of the boat. Cold water took my breath away, and I had my first and only encounter with a "keeper hole" that refused to release me. A keeper hole is where water swirls, turns on itself, and spins you around and around like a washing machine, making it almost impossible to break away from its power. Jay's buddy, who worked as a guide on the Colorado River, pulled up beside me. I grabbed onto the back of his boat and he pulled me towards shore. Gripped with fear, I waded through knee-deep water until I reached the edge of the bank. I clambered up the steep embankment through Slide Alder, a nightmare to hike through. An hour later I came out onto a road in what felt like the middle of nowhere. Disoriented, I had no idea how I would find the "romantic adventurer" who had gotten me into this mess. Wet, cold, and lost, I stormed down the road. A lady came by and picked me up, thankfully, since I was nearly hypothermic from the winter chill. She knew where kayakers usually parked when they paddled the river, so she graciously let me drip-dry in her car as she drove me to the parking lot. I waited for what felt like an eternity before I saw Jay and his other friends pulling out of the river. We exchanged some nasty words and I vowed never to speak with him again.

That first date was a foretaste of our future partnership, where one adventure after another turned into a calamity of errors. Boredom never entered our lives as we seized every opportunity for exploring and discovering. We loved deeply and fought like tigers. Against all odds, we vowed to spend the rest of our lives together. Life moved too quickly for us to keep up. Three months after our first date, I became pregnant with my firstborn, Zach, and Jay received notice that he had to be in Gold River within weeks to start his job with Western Forest Products. He left a month before me because I wanted to finish my job as a teacher on call with the Vancouver School District. A month later, with trepidation, I packed everything I owned into my little Firefly and left for Gold River, a tiny village on the west side of Vancouver Island.

Gold River took some time to adapt to after living in Kitsilano, a funky little Vancouver suburb. Life in the city, though chaotic, always had interesting places to explore and new things to see: coffee shops, restaurants, bookstores, theatres, and galleries. Every nook and cranny had something to be discovered. Each day after school, my roommates and I quickly updated one another on the details of our day, and then I would lace up my running shoes and run along the seawall, taking in the smells and sounds of the ocean. Within the safety of our home, the three of us shared our innermost thoughts, hopes, dreams, and fears. We laughed until we cried and cried until we laughed. After settling in Gold River, I missed my roommates' presence in my day-to-day life. I was not used to the isolation and loneliness of a small logging community without my two closest friends.

Paying off student loans left Jay and I struggling financially, so we lived in a run-down apartment called the Gold Crest, locally known as the Projects or the "Mold Crest." Once we had saved some money, we moved into a tiny condo and life became much more bearable. After many months of loneliness and hormonal upheaval due to my pregnancy, I finally met some friends who became my closest companions and supporters. Kate, Cheryl, Corrine, and I did everything together—running, hiking, rock climbing, mountain biking, and everything in between. We spent many of our days hiking the beautiful trails of Strathcona Park and swimming in the stunning Gold River that flowed through the middle of town. Believe it or not, Jay and I still kayaked together and would often go out on long summer days when he got home from work. As long as I could fit into my kayak, we paddled together. Six months into my pregnancy, I could no longer squeeze my oversized body into the cockpit, so we had to find other, less challenging ways to entertain ourselves.

In place of wild adventures, I began to appreciate long hikes and deep conversations with my friend Kate. When we were together, she occasionally brought up Jesus in conversation, and we would talk about Christianity. She was not pushy or edgy. She just lovingly told me about the one who had changed her life. Kate modelled Jesus' love well, so I was willing to listen to her. Eventually, she invited Jay and I to an Alpha course, a ten-day introduction to the basics of the Christian faith. There, we made the decision to follow Jesus. It was a wobbly decision, but a decision nonetheless. The loving, merciful God Jay and I learned about in this course was much different than the God I remembered from my childhood. Even so, it would be a long time before we understood Jesus' expansive love for us. At this point in our decision, our hearts could not comprehend that he loved us in the midst of our mess. It felt too good to be true.

Having special friends who cared about us emotionally and spiritually eased the loneliness so I could enjoy my pregnancy more. Aside from being enormous, I had no complications whatsoever. I tried to stay active in spite of my size. One afternoon, riding my bike along a logging road, one of the Jay's coworkers called him on his truck radio, laughing his head off. He said, "Jay, Dana is riding her bike down the road and she looks like a frog." My stomach made it impossible for my legs to go up and down, so they had to go side to side. When Jay came home from work and told me the story, I decided to hang up my bike until after my pregnancy. I could not even walk for long periods of time due to the pressure on my bladder. I would walk a block and then have to bolt for the bushes to do my business. Finally, my stomach got so large I had to buy a very unattractive full body harness, which crisscrossed around the back and cinched my stomach up to relieve the abdominal pressure. I was a sight to behold. With only a few weeks left in my pregnancy, I was dreadfully uncomfortable. My skin had stretched in ways I thought were impossible. The only way I could find any comfort was by rubbing tubes of calamine lotion all over my belly. I thought the itching was going to make me insane. Hot, constricted, and terribly itchy, I was not fun to be around.

My due date was at the end of December 1996, so in the middle of the month, we prepared to go to Kamloops where our families could support us during and after the birth. I predicted Zach would be early, but to our dismay and frustration, he was born two weeks late. Finally, with a massive amount of black hair, unusually dark eyes, and eight pounds of cuteness, Zachary Schylore Laird entered the world at Royal Inland Hospital. Jay and I felt a wide range of emotions after Zach's birth. Mostly we were overjoyed, but we also felt inept. After hours of trying to comfort Zach I felt exasperated. Occasionally babies get their days and nights mixed up when they are born and Zach seemed to sleep all day and cry all night. While Zach fussed in his bassinet, I rocked myself in a corner, sleep deprived and overwhelmed. Jay read *What To Expect When You're Expecting* with his flashlight, hoping to find out why our beautiful baby boy would not stop crying. With sudden revelation, Jay looked up from his reading and said, "Babe, I know what's wrong! He is cluster feeding to stimulate more milk supply. It's normal! There is nothing wrong with him." Jay knew I was on the verge of insanity, so he took Zach and rocked him all night, bringing him to me only when he needed feeding. Jay and

I were blindsided by the demands of having a newborn. I am not sure what we thought it would be like, but it had not occurred to us that we would not sleep *at all.*

The temperature in Kamloops had dropped to minus twenty degrees Celsius, so we were confined to the indoors. In the blur of doing laundry, changing diapers, breast-feeding and sleepless nights, I was going a bit crazy. I needed to get outside, breathe in fresh air, exercise and have time to collect my thoughts. But dressing a baby for cold temperatures was another challenge. I found it awkward to fit Zach's tiny limbs into his doll-sized clothes, and the production of getting his winter attire on was an event that needed to be scheduled into the calendar. Jay was much better at dressing Zach, but he had gone back home to Gold River to catch up on work. I was left alone for our first outdoor winter adventure. I quickly realized I should have bundled Zach up after I had figured out how to piece together the Snuggly. By the time I understood how all the straps and snaps worked, Zach was screaming uncontrollably. Finally, after an hour of preparation, we ventured out into the cold. Zach settled into sleep, but after only twenty minutes of walking I realized I had to go to the bathroom. I panicked at the thought of what this huge inconvenience meant. I ran, ever so gently, trying not to wake him as I made a beeline to the mall to use the washroom. Once in the tiny stall, I fumbled impatiently with all the snuggly gadgets, horrifically aware I might not actually make it. My mind buzzed. *Why was such a simple thing so difficult? What would I do once I had the carrier off? Should I lay him on the floor? Hang him on the hook? Put him in the sink?* Pandemonium broke out in the stall and it dawned on me that simple things would never be simple again. For two weeks, I stayed with my mom and her husband Ray to get my bearings before they drove me back to Gold River at the end of January. A typical eight-hour trip turned into a fourteen-hour ordeal. Zach slept intermittently, but mostly he cried. We would go a short distance and then have to stop to rock and feed Zach or change his diaper. Travelling with a baby was torture.

Slowly, after a clumsy beginning adjusting to our new life, Jay and I settled into our new role as parents. My life felt rich and complete in the midst of the chaos. I felt a love and warmth I never imagined possible. Two years later, on April 19, 1999, our second son Carter entered our lives. Unlike Zach, he came earlier than expected and almost arrived on the windy, single lane highway linking Gold River to Campbell River. My water broke in Gold River, so we quickly drove Zach to the babysitter and climbed into our rusty, unreliable Subaru to begin our one-and-a-half-hour drive to Campbell River. Jay's calm, never-get-frazzled personality exasperated me. He drove below the speed limit, while I anticipated I would have Carter on the side of the road. I finally screamed, "Pull the car over and let me drive!" When I finally scrambled out of the car and walked toward the hospital, I had to squat to walk because I was convinced Carter was going to drop out onto the road. Two hours after arriving at the Campbell River Hospital, my blonde-haired, blue-eyed Carter Daniel Laird entered our lives, four ounces heavier than his older brother at birth. Because we were more calm the second time around, Carter was content. He loved to snuggle and rarely stopped smiling. Our whole family delighted in him. Zach hovered over him like a mother hen, bending to his every need. Right from the beginning, they shared a special bond. Carter would utter sounds and Zach would interpret them. Carter did not learn to talk for a very long time because Zach spoke for him. Almost one hundred percent of the time, Zach knew exactly what his brother was communicating.

After a few years in Gold River, Western Forest Products offered Jay a promotion as a resident engineer in Zeballos. With some reluctance, we both agreed the move would be a smart financial decision. After two years of living in Zeballos we would have our student loans and the rest of our debt paid off. In August 2001, we left Gold River and moved to the small isolated village on the northwest coast of Vancouver Island. Zeballos had a population of about 250 people, including the Ehhattesat First Nations population. It is situated at the head of Zeballos Inlet, the gateway to Nootka Sound, and is world famous for salmon fishing and kayaking. Zeballos was a whole new level of isolation. Port McNeil, our only place to get groceries, involved a one-and-a-half-hour drive along a bumpy, dusty, and treacherous logging road. We would often meet oncoming logging trucks and have to back our Subaru to the closest pullout, not an easy task with cliffs on either side and two babies demanding attention. The rugged beauty of the place with its surrounding old growth forest and mountains stood in contrast to the dilapidated buildings and hurting people. Houses lay in ruins, some half built and others decaying due to all the rain. Child abuse, neglect, juvenile delinquency, and substance abuse created a thick and oppressive atmosphere. During our time there, I had very little support raising Zach and Carter. Family lived so far away and Jay usually worked seventy hours a week. To battle depression, I would run like a lunatic on the bumpy logging roads. I had a double baby jogger and, rain or shine, we would hit the road for an hour and a half so I could get high on endorphins. I brought lots of food along so that whenever the boys started to fight, I would toss granola bars, cheerios, and other little tidbits through the hole in the top of the jogger. Once in a while, they would start screaming, and I would look through the peephole to find them stretching each other's lips or pinching one another. We would stop to watch the dump trucks and loaders at the dryland log sort as a reward for not pinching, biting, hitting, or yelling while in the baby jogger.

Despite the challenges of rural isolation, our family enjoyed fishing adventures in the inlet where we would jig for cod and throw down prawn traps, praying our decrepit boat would not fail us. Every day, we would put on rain gear and go on some sort of adventure — puddle jumping, golfing balls into the ocean and then going to collect them at low tide, looking for weird creatures in the tidal pools, riding bikes, or going to the playground. On the occasional day when it was not raining, the boys liked to go out on the deck and paint in the nude. That way, they could paint with abandon. We would set them loose with globs of paint and rolled out paper and they would go to work. Once they were covered from head to toe with rainbows of colour, Jay would hook up the hose to the hot water tank and spray them off.

Even though Jay worked long hours, he always made time for his boys. He would come home and connect with them before heading back to work after they went to bed. The stress of his work responsibilities left little time to rest and take in life, but carving out time for Zach and Carter was a priority for him. From the time he got home until the boys went to bed, it was fun time with dad. I loved listening to the squealing in the house when Jay got home from work. Zach and Carter would hear his truck pull into the driveway and bound to the window. I would open it as Jay yelled, "Bring me those boys!" I would lower them through the window and he would pile them into the company truck, go to the candy store, and take them to the office so they could use his stamps and watch the dump trucks and loaders at the dryland sort. Jay's favourite time to connect with the boys was after dinner. He took over bedtime routines and the three of them had a circuit they would do each night. After water fights in the bathroom, he would pull each boy out of the tub and yell, "Who wants to jump in the towel?" Giggles would erupt, followed by excited shrieks, "Me! Pick me first!" The bathroom door would fly open and he would have one of them yelling, "Higher, daddy! Bounce me higher!" He would bounce them, wrapped in towels, all over the house like kangaroos. Following the kangaroo act, he would invite them to a wrestling match. We could not afford a bed, so the mattress on the floor made the perfect arena. After their wrestling, jumping and pile drives, he would squish them between pillows, a game they called "pillow sandwich." Their boisterous play was their way of attaching.

For one year we made the best of our situation. Jay's stress was unhealthy. The demands of his work were at an all-time high and we felt the effects of his long working hours on our relationship. He made sure his boys' needs were met, but there was little time for us. Even though we were burdened by Jay's long working hours, I agreed to a part-time teaching contract with the school to relieve some of our financial load. Although the break from the daily toddler routine felt good, I was pushed in too many directions. Many of the children and teens I worked with had fetal alcohol syndrome and I was teaching all subjects from grade six to grade ten, which left me feeling exhausted at the end of the day. I would run on my lunch hour at school just so I could cope with the chaos of work. I knew if I ran before I went home, I would be able to connect with my family in a healthier way. Jay had no way of relieving his stress because he worked continuously. Both Jay and I were stretched too far. However, knowing Jay's job would soon come to an end and we would be able to leave Zeballos before Zach started kindergarten kept us from drowning in stress.

We have troubles all around us, but we are not defeated.

We do not know what to do, but we do not give up the hope of living.

We are persecuted, but God does not leave us.

We are hurt sometimes, but we are not destroyed.

—2 Corinthians 8-9 (NCV)

CHAPTER 2

STUMBLING IN THE DARK

"At that moment I needed prayer as much as I needed air to draw my breath or oxygen to fill my blood…a void was behind me. And in front a wall, a wall of darkness."

—George Bernanos

At twenty-five, one month before we began dating, Jay had a large lump removed from his shoulder. After a biopsy, doctors had told him it was cancerous, but what Jay did not know was that the tumour was an aggressive sarcoma, likely to come back within five years. He had assumed after surgery he was cancer free. On a summer afternoon in 1995, Jay and I had spent the afternoon sea kayaking near Granville Island in Vancouver. After a relaxing day and a quiet dinner, Jay started to feel some pain in his arm and it began to swell at an alarming rate. At first, we thought he had overdone it at the gym, but we soon realized the problem seemed much more serious than simply overexertion. We went to the emergency room at Vancouver General Hospital, where he was admitted for tests. After a painful process of inserting dye into his arm, doctors discovered he had deep vein thrombosis (DVT). DVT happens when a blood clot forms in the deep veins. The condition can be deadly if a clot breaks loose, travels through the bloodstream and lodges into the lungs, potentially causing a pulmonary embolism. Later, we discovered DVT in young people is often an indicator of cancer. Jay's symptoms foreshadowed the dark path we would walk in the near future.

Near the end of our first year in Zeballos in 2001, Jay started experiencing health problems again. He seemed tired and unusually lethargic. After days in the bush surveying, he would come home complaining of being out of shape and short of breath. He thought he should cut down on coffee because of his chronic headaches, which he attributed to stress. His health continued to worsen. Adding to the fatigue, he had unbearable back pain. He could not roughhouse with the kids anymore because his pain was too intense. In the middle of October, he began to take muscle relaxants to ease the back pain, but still he could not get the pain under control. All the symptoms culminated in the middle of the night on October 20th. Screaming in agony, Jay could not breathe. His lungs had filled up with fluid and he was wracked with pain. He tried to calm himself with a warm shower, but the pain did not subside for the rest of the night. Early the next morning he left for the Port McNeil Hospital.

Jay called me during the day and said hospital staff were admitting him overnight for tests. Doctors needed to drain fluid off his lungs before transferring him the following day to Campbell River for further testing. My heart felt heavy as I packed a few things into the car the next day. Just as the boys and I were about to leave, it dawned on me to pack their Halloween costumes even though it was only the middle of October. I sensed we would not be returning for a while. The boys fooled around in the back seat of the car, unaware their life was about to change forever. I glanced in the rearview mirror at the scenery behind me as we drove away. In my heart, I said goodbye to what I was leaving behind. By the time we got to the hospital, my uneasiness had escalated into full-blown fear. As soon as I saw Jay, my tears flowed. I asked the nurses if they thought his symptoms might be cancer-related. One nurse, not knowing Jay's cancer history, assured me his age and health made him an unlikely candidate. My dreadful premonition, though, already had me wondering how I would live without him.

After blood work and a CT scan at the Campbell River Hospital, doctors confirmed what I had feared: Jay had cancer. As the news settled, Zach fidgeted with his Lego transformer, trying to distract himself from our tears and his own distress. At four years old he knew something was horrifically wrong. Carter, only two years old, seemed unaware that our world was being ripped apart. In the middle of our upheaval, a doctor handed us an envelope that we were to give to the oncologist upon arriving at Royal Jubilee Hospital in Victoria. In a fog, we all left the waiting room, walked out into the night and made our way to our hotel. As I settled the boys into bed, dread rolled in with such fierce power that I felt out of control. Nothing I tried would calm my heart so I drove back to the ER to get a prescription for Ativan. I slipped the tiny pill under my tongue and let it take me to a place of numbness.

The next day we got up early, had a quick breakfast and drove to Sooke, a small community on the outskirts of Victoria. Jay's pain raged. Doctors had not prescribed pain medication, so he had to endure the drive with nothing to ease his symptoms. My loyal Gold River friend, Kate, had arranged a place in Sooke where we could stay for the duration of Jay's treatments. My mom and Ray met us there and as soon as I saw them, I felt relief for the first time in a week. My mom stilled my heart. We followed my her and Ray to our homey cabin tucked in the forest. Kate had filled the fridge with groceries so we did not have to worry ourselves with overwhelming day-to-day errands. My mom, Ray, and Jay's mom and dad, Maureen and Skye, were able to stay in two empty cabins beside us.

The day after arriving in Sooke, we had an appointment with an oncologist in Victoria to go over the results of Jay's scans. As soon as she came into the room, I knew we were in trouble. Her eyes looked heavy with regret. Quietly, she started to speak, as if the softness in her voice could protect us from the severity of the news she was about to deliver. Her words ambushed us. She got right to the point: Jay had six months to live. A biopsy confirmed he had a rare, aggressive soft tissue sarcoma called malignant fibroid histiocytoma. Silence reverberated in the room. The clock ticked but time stood still. I felt like we had been sucked into a black abyss. I retreated behind a curtain of numbness, walking out to the waiting room where my mom, Ray, Margie, Maureen, Skye and Kate were waiting. There was no gentle way to say it, so I just said, "Jay has six months to live." The words seemed to be coming out of someone else's mouth. The moment felt detached and surreal. Light-headed with night-marish thoughts, I could not imagine how our family would survive.

Jay's chemotherapy treatments were brutal. We would drive in every day to Royal Jubilee for chemotherapy infusions. Jay's hair began to fall out and he started losing substantial amounts of weight. Balancing his pain medications seemed like a losing battle. We could not stay on top of it. He would sleep on and off twenty-four hours a day. The only thing that woke him up was pain. His emotions ebbed and flowed. Soft emotions like sadness and gentleness would give way to jagged emotions like anger and bitterness. Jay grieved over his loss of identity. How he had defined himself had changed overnight. He also grieved over what his illness was doing to his family. Both of us mourned for how our lives were falling apart. My own sorrow became so intense it felt as though I had a disorder or a disease. If I had experienced this type of pain at any other time in my life, I would have admitted myself to the psychiatric ward. Life had been reduced to hospital visits, blood work, ER visits and sickness. Days of laughter and adventures were over. Jay lost about forty pounds and most days I could tell he just wished it could be over. Many days I yearned for it to be over, too. I wished the disease would take him quickly so we would not have to watch his slow death. Fear of suffering for a long time was at the forefront of our thoughts.

During the weeks of Jay's treatments, my family's support got us through some of the saddest moments of our lives. My mom prepared meals for us and made sure we had clean laundry every day. She took over the small tasks that somehow seemed mammoth, so my attention could rest on caring for my family. Margie entertained the boys with hot chocolate, hikes and pool adventures. She filled in for my absence. She created a collage of our family to hang on the wall as a reminder of the love that bound us together. Knowing how much I found comfort in reading and journaling, Margie gave me a gift bag with a journal and grief books by Elizabeth Kubler Ross as well as children's books on grief. Each night, she would massage my feet while listening to the pain in my heart.

After Jay had one month of treatments at Royal Jubilee, we all returned to our hometown of Kamloops, where my mom and Ray had secured a condo for us to move into as soon as we arrived from Victoria. After only a two-week respite from his treatments in Victoria, Jay started three months of treatments in Kelowna. He would have one week of treatments and three weeks off. His first round of chemotherapy began on November 30th, 2001, and his last treatment would be on February 20th, 2002. During his weeks off, Jay would conjure up all his strength to play with his boys. He found getting out of bed torturous some days, yet he wanted to spend his last months creating good memories with his sons. But just when Jay would start to feel human again, he would have to go in for another round of treatments. Then he would be bedridden for two weeks until his blood cell count went back up again, usually around the beginning of week three.

In between treatments, just before Christmas, Pastor Lamont Schmidt from Valleyview Bible Church came to our home to deliver a poinsettia and introduce himself. Our pastor in Gold River had told him about our family. Pastor Lamont wanted to connect with us so we did not feel alone in the community. Instantly, I sensed his love. He was not afraid of our situation. Terminal cancer did not scare him off. He genuinely cared about the details going on in our lives, and encouraged us to come to church the following Sunday. Before leaving, he shared a verse from the Bible he believed God wanted to give us. For the first time, I heard the verse that would become one of my favourites: "He will cover you with his feathers. He will shelter you with his wings. His faithful promises are your armor and protection" (Psalm 94:1) As soon as the words left his mouth I felt peace. This moment was a pivotal point on our faith journey. Had Pastor Lamont not stepped out in love to show his support, I highly doubt Jay and I would have attended church in Kamloops. Our faith was still relatively fresh and a storm of this magnitude could have easily ripped up our newly established spiritual roots.

We attended church that Sunday and met a few people in the congregation who seemed kind and inviting. Pastor Lamont wanted to connect us to a care group in Juniper Ridge, close to where we lived, but Jay and I decided we would rather keep to ourselves. Within a week, we received a message on our voicemail from a woman named Laurie Simonin, who personally invited us to her care group. We erased the message and did not phone her back. We kept screening her calls, hoping she would stop calling. Finally, Jay said, "Let's just call her back. Maybe she will stop phoning us." So, I called her. I felt badly telling her we did not want to come, so I ended up making plans to attend the next week. Jay got the same look on his face he always got when I talked him into things he did not want to do.

The last time I had seen that look of exasperation was when I talked him into doing a downhill mountain bike race with me at Sun Peaks. We had shown up with lame bikes, no armor and outdated helmets. When we went to buy our race plates, it was all the guy selling them to us could do to contain his laughter. "You guys can't be serious. You can't go in the race unless you have armor. It is mandatory," he said. So, we rented armor and paid money we could not afford to go in a race that was horrifying in every way. After the trial run, Jay gave me the silent treatment. Our performance was an embarrassment. With a great amount of humiliation, Jay finished and then waited at the bottom for me. I had actually done quite well, considering my bike was a piece of junk, until my chain bounced off my derailleur and jammed. Looking down to see what the problem was, I flew off the trail, going over my handlebars and careening down a bank. I limped back up the bank with blood dripping down my legs, only to realize I had a flat tire. Mortified, I walked the rest of the way down, only to face Jay's disapproving glare at the finish line. Now, as I shared the news about going to a Bible study, he gave me the same look.

We dreaded going to the care group. Both of us felt vulnerable and worried that socializing would sap any energy we still had left. But, surprisingly, soon after arriving at one of the member's homes, we felt at ease. The group's kindness overwhelmed both of us. When people prayed for us, I felt a strange peace come over me that was unfamiliar. Jay and I had never prayed out loud before, so it was terribly awkward when each person prayed in turn around a circle. There was a deafening silence when our turn came to pray. It felt so uncomfortable that neither of us had the courage to speak up. People quickly filled in the silence so we would not feel embarrassed. Slowly, after a few months of attending this group, praying out loud became slightly more natural. Pray became central to our emotional health. Whenever we would leave for treatments in Kelowna, I would feel our friends' prayers back home. I could sense them lifting us up faithfully. This beautiful group of people showed Jay and I God's tangible love. Without their support of meals, prayers, and care, it is very likely I would not be walking with God today. Prayers at our care group felt powerful and I started to think Jay might be healed. Pastor Lamont called together a church meeting where family and friends gathered around Jay to pray for a miracle. I had hope that something was going to change, but weeks after the gathering, Jay's health took a drastic turn for the worse.

As Jay deteriorated, my heart ached for Zach and Carter. They witnessed their playful, energetic daddy dying a little more each day. They were confused, afraid, and desperately sad. I wanted to pull them away and protect them from watching Jay's suffering up close. Cancer tainted their childhood. At a young age, they had to learn how the world is full of unfathomable pain. I could not protect them. I had to let them be part of this pain. Grief was part of the healing journey, but it felt so wrong. The boys should have been going on outings, exploring the wonders of their world, delighting in the sweetness of childhood, and rough housing with their dad. But, over time, Jay spent less time playing and more time in bed. He still liked to read bedtime stories to his boys, so Zach and Carter would snuggle in with him after a bath and read their favourite books. They loved to paint pictures for Jay, which we taped above his bed to cheer him.

Jay's condition continued to worsen until, finally, we had to make the decision about whether to put him in hospice or take care of him at home. Jay's mom had a nursing background, so we decided together to take care of him at home. Images of the dying process haunted all of us. The sounds of dying were the most traumatizing—the gurgling of life draining, the slow agonizing breaths, and the horrible stench of death stealing the one we loved. The tumour pressed in on Jay's voice box so he could not communicate with us verbally. To comfort him, I would sing or hum as a way to soothe him and keep our fear at bay. Jay and I had listened to singer Loreena McKennit a lot when we were dating, so I hummed her song "Greensleeves." I knew it would comfort him. He seemed less agitated whenever I hummed. For a few days, we communicated this way, but soon, he became unresponsive. Yet, when he heard the sound of his boys, he would jolt awake, defying death. He could not bear the thought of leaving them. As soon as he heard Zach and Carter's laughter, he longed to stay with them so he could protect and take care of them.

On the evening of July 14th, 2002, at only thirty-years-old, Jay died. A sun set in the sky more beautiful than I had ever seen. Zach and Carter lay down beside their dad one last time, touching him and saying their goodbyes. Maureen put fresh clothes on Jay, removed all of the intravenous lines and gently touched and held her son. Sadly, I do not remember what I did. I must have gone on autopilot to take care of arrangements with the funeral home. I managed to dissociate from my pain in order to do what needed to be done. My mom and Ray came by the condo to pick up the boys and I. When the doctor came to announce Jay's death and the funeral home came to take his body, I could not bear the thought of being in the house alone. I remember being cold and shivery when my mom and Ray came to get us. My body was in shock.

Days after Jay's death, I found two opposing emotions warring inside of me: relief and a deep, indescribable sorrow. Caregiving had taken its toll and there had been no rest along the way. Most nights, Jay had been up all night in pain. On especially bad nights, I had sometimes fantasized about it all being over. On several occasions, Jay and the boys had been sick at the same time, so I had taken care of everyone. But no matter how overwhelmed, sad, or angry I had been, I felt I did not have the right to such feelings. After all, Jay was the one with cancer. *Who was I to complain?* I had thought. During those days, I tried to bury all my pain. Depression lingered because there seemed to be no end in sight. I felt guilty that part of me was looking forward to having some of my freedom back. Some days I was angry that Jay would be lucky enough to die. When he was in paradise, I would still have to sort through this earthly mess. I had tried to clamp the lid down on these dark thoughts, but they would push back with greater force. For those who have never been a caregiver for a loved one during a terminal illness, thoughts like these may seem strange and cold. But to those who have been a caregiver over the long haul, these mixed up feelings are normal and even understandable.

My brief sense of relief after Jay's death, though, left within a week. After that, I ached to have him back. My heart shrivelled from loneliness, especially on days when the boys were at school. The void was horrendously painful. Never again would Jay take part in our family's day-to-day lives. Never again would he snuggle his boys while reading bedtime stories. Never again would we go on crazy adventures together. Never again would he sit at the table with us. He would never see his children graduate from high school or marry. For the rest of our lives we would have to navigate life without him. The emptiness felt unendurable.

I was intentional about reading everything I could get my hands on to help Zach and Carter process their grief. In one of Carter's play therapy sessions, he shared his fear that I was going to die, too. We cuddled lots and read books addressing the process of grief, including *The Fall of Freddie the Leaf*, *When the Wind Stops*, *Badger's Parting Gifts*, and *Gentle Willow*. These books explored sadness, disbelief, and anger, along with tools of healing such as love, compassion, and caregiving. Using simple language, these stories helped Zach and Carter find their way through their sadness. We also intentionally remembered Jay by talking about him often, making collages, sleeping with his shirts, and making scrapbooks of our times we had shared together. I wished I could get into their minds to better understand their hearts. I watched for every indicator that they were not doing well, but, amazingly, they seemed well adjusted considering the magnitude of what they had been through.

Longing for joy again shortly after Jay died, the boys and I went on a road trip to Kananaskis in the Canadian Rockies to visit Margie and my niece, Saige. We went hiking and biking and soaked in the healing balm of nature. The smell of fresh air, the sounds of streams, and the majesty of the mountains were therapeutic and refreshing for our worn-out souls. I identified with John Muir, Sierra Club's founder, who writes of how we can "climb the mountains to get their good tidings. Nature's peace will flow into [us] as sunshine flows into trees. The winds will blow their own freshness into [us], and the storms their energy, while cares will drop off like autumn leaves."[1] For me, nature drew me closer to God. It took me back to my younger years of simplicity. I could feel God's peace, and I felt whole and more connected. Trauma had left me walking around disconnected from myself, but in nature, it felt like a black curtain lifted, and I could see in colour again.

For a long time after Jay's death, life ebbed and flowed, full colour one moment and then dark night the next. I called it the grief dance. I learned how to move with the tide of grief instead of resisting it. A smell, a greeting card, a movie or a familiar song would send me into spasms of pain. Many nights I cried what felt like gallons of tears into my pillow. At times, I would wake up alone in the dark and twitches of anxiety would keep me awake until morning. Some days I felt nothing and wondered what was wrong with me. Other days I felt happy and would realize with a jolt I had not thought of Jay for most of the day. Emotional confusion lingered in the air long after Jay died. Sometimes anger, resentment, and bitterness crept in, along with guilt over not being as emotionally available to Zach and Carter as I wanted to be. I felt guilty when I would explode at inappropriate times, hurting my children with my impatience. I began to accept that confusing, intense, and sometimes weird emotions were my new normal. Gradually, life gained momentum, and I became ready to emerge from my long winter of grieving.

Jay, Zach, Carter and myself in Gold River

Carter resting after a long day in the mountains

*Hanging out in beautiful Kananaskis Country after a day
of hiking with Auntie Margie and Saige*

More adventures together in Kananaskis

*Taking a break to play at the park during
the time Jay was sick*

Look at the new thing I am going to do.

It is already happening. Don't you see it?

I will make a road in the desert and rivers in the dry land.

—Isaiah 43:19 (NCV)

Chapter 3

New Beginnings

Take the first step of faith. You don't have to see the whole
staircase, just take the first step.

— Martin Luther King, Jr.

At the time Jay died, I never considered finding someone else — I
just wanted him. I never expected to find another person I could
love as much as I had loved Jay. But, one year after Jay's death, life and
love unfolded naturally. A man named Doug attended my church, and
we would talk occasionally after the service over coffee. Doug had experienced his own cancer journey that had run nearly parallel to my own.
He understood this pilgrimage through pain. His wife, Kathy, had died
of ovarian cancer six months before Jay had passed away. Doug's family,
like mine, had faced cancer and now lived in its ugly wake. The clouds
of sorrow and grief lay low over his family, too. Doug had two children,
Darcie, his eighteen-year-old daughter, who was in nursing school at
Thomson Rivers University, and Ryan, his twenty-year-old son, who was

at Simon Fraser University working on his bachelor's degree. Darcie and Ryan were learning how to function in their personal and academic lives while carrying the pain of losing their mom. Typically, moms know their children better than anyone else, intuitively understanding their hearts, loving them unconditionally, and protecting them from injustice. From what Doug shared with me about Kathy, I learned she was that kind of a mother. The ache in Darcie and Ryan's hearts must have been bottomless.

In the middle of December 2003, Doug and I finally agreed to go for coffee outside of church. We were not officially calling it a date, but it was a step towards greater connection. Soon, the Christmas season began to weigh heavily on both of us. To escape, Doug decided to take his children, along with Darcie's best friend, Kirsten, to Kauai. I wished I could escape, too, from the painful reminders of the not so distant past, but I knew my memories and emotions would follow me wherever I went. Grief will not let you take shortcuts. Our first Christmas without Jay was empty and hollow. Before life had been tainted with death, Christmas was my favourite time of year, but now it felt flat, only serving to remind me of Jay's absence. The empty chair at our kitchen table churned up deep wells of grief in me. Memories of Jay were frustrating, poor substitutes for the real thing. I tried to recall details of Christmases past by looking at photos, but snapshots are one-dimensional and colourless. Pictures do not breathe or talk. I could only imagine what his hair felt like, or how his voice sounded, but I would never actually touch his hair or hear his voice again. Specific conversations or moments of laughter were reduced to made-up versions in my imagination. The truth was I struggled to remember the details of so much of our lives together. What I did remember seemed out of focus and unfulfilling. However, for Zach and Carter's sake, I exaggerated the Christmas spirit to make up for the ache in our hearts.

When Doug returned from Kauai in January, we occasionally connected for a night run or dinner. Gradually, we began to spend more and more time together. We enjoyed mountain biking, skiing, running, watching movies and talking into the wee hours of the night. We never ran out of things to talk about and I loved his company. Even though we enjoyed being together, Doug seemed a bit reluctant about our relationship, so I decided to test it out. He had sung Mercy Me's song, "I Can Only Imagine" during a recent service at Valleyview Bible Church and his voice moved me. So, I invited him for coffee and slipped two tickets to a Joe Cocker concert into Mercy Me's book, *I Can Only Imagine.* There was only one stipulation: he had to take me to the concert. That moment was the tipping point for taking our relationship to the next level.

Doug introduced me to the finer things in life. After I had spent three years in logging towns, fancy did not register on my radar. One evening, Doug phoned me and told me to dress up because he was taking me somewhere special. To me, dressing up meant wearing my clean pair of Birkenstocks. Doug arrived in a suit and tie, probably flabbergasted that I looked like Laura Ingalls Wilder from *Little House On the Praires.* He did not say anything, but a few weeks later he took me shopping for some fancy things to add to my wardrobe. One night I attempted to blow his mind with my fanciness and bought a pair of high heels for our dinner at the Keg. The hostess took us up a flight of stairs and as we sat, I was painfully aware that eventually I would need to go back down those stairs. Partway through dinner, I had to go to the bathroom. Slowly and painfully I made my way to the washroom. Doug realized how much of an effort the ordeal was for me, and from that day on, he would keep a vice grip on me whenever I wore high heels.

Doug had many qualities pretty special in a man. He took time to plan out-of-the-ordinary dates. When we went mountain biking, he would put together a picnic, complete with Asiago cheese, Starbucks coffee and chocolate. He loved planning dinners, playing music, and being romantic. He had an eye for decorating and taught me to appreciate art. He also had a gift for serving. One time, I went away on a trip to

Vancouver Island with my friends, and when I got home, my grass was cut and a welcome home note was scribed on my driveway with sidewalk chalk. For this single mom, these practical and romantic gestures moved me deeply. Although all of these special characteristics drew me to him, one date sealed the deal. He phoned me to say he was taking me on an unusual adventure and I needed to wear old clothes. I had no idea what to expect. We pulled into an unfamiliar place, he grabbed Perrier water out of the trunk of his car, and we made our way toward an old building. Because Doug was a firefighter, he had permission to use the firefighter's training center where they practice live burn exercises. A few other firefighters had their families there as well. He handed me my turnout gear and a breathing apparatus and told me to gear up: we were going into a burning building. I could hardly move in the heavy gear and I had to battle claustrophobia when I put on my helmet and breathing apparatus. Doug ignited the building and we went in. I held the front of the hose and Doug followed behind. The heat from the fire felt intense. Doug told me to douse the flames with short bursts of water to knock down the fire and cool the temperature. I loved the thrill! This event was a perfect example of how Doug satiated my desire for romance and adventure.

From our time together, I felt certain Doug would be a man who would maximize togetherness in our family. He integrated Zach and Carter into his life and cared about what they cared about. He knew how to have fun and brought the sparkle back into my boys' eyes. Zach called me into his room one night, concerned he might love Doug as much as he loved his dad, and this reassured me that Doug had established a powerful heart connection with my boys. Doug opened doors for me, spoke with tenderness, valued my feelings, and considered my thoughts on things. These were all qualities I wanted modelled to my sons. His considerate ways assured me he would show Zach and Carter how to be honourable men.

Before Jay died, he promised me I would find someone really special to be a father to Zach and Carter. Doug exceeded my expectations.

In December 2003, after six months of dating, Doug and I went to Margie's place in Banff for a get-away. There, he proposed to me under a Christmas tree at the Banff Springs Hotel. His proposal felt like a winter fairytale. So much had changed in one year. Our previous Christmas had been coloured in pain; this season held meaning, infused with romance and love. My ring was simple, elegant and beautiful. Darcie had helped Doug pick it out, which meant a lot to me. I am sure she had mixed feelings of pain and joy about her dad marrying someone else, yet she lovingly chose to be involved in our relationship. Both Ryan and Darcie had welcomed the boys and I into their lives. On March 6th, 2004, we were married at Sun Rivers in Kamloops. Our wedding was quite small, with only a few close friends and family. Zach and Carter were ring bearers, looking utterly handsome in their suits. My niece, Saige, lined the stairs with rose petals as I walked toward Doug, who waited for me with Ryan, Darcie, Zach, Carter, and Margie beside him. Singer and songwriter Heather Clark sang "Kisses of Your Mouth," and "I Am My Beloved's and He is Mine," songs based on Song of Solomon, a book in the Bible celebrating love between a husband and a wife. I was completely filled with joy as I joined hands with Doug. After a few words from our pastor, Dan Warkentin, Doug had a surprise for me. He sang Bryan Adam's song, "I'll Always Be Right There," while Heather played the piano. Looking into Doug's eyes as he sang, I knew he would be there for me no matter what happened on our journey together.

Before we married, we had chosen a home in upper Sahali. We were excited to move in and begin our new lives together. After a few weeks of setting up our home, we left for our honeymoon in Bermuda. The night before we left, I cried on and off throughout the night because I had never been apart from my boys. I was excited to get away, but uneasy at the same time. Once on the plane, though, I began to relax. I had never been to a tropical paradise, so when we landed in Bermuda, I was stunned by the beauty. Right away, we rented a scooter and Doug showed me around the island. The expansive beaches and rich blue waters were breathtaking. The pink talc-like sand is formed from finely pulverized remains of corals, clams, forams and other shells and it feels like flour. We spent hours running along the beaches early in the mornings. During the day, we snorkeled, swam, sailed and biked around the island. Our honeymoon was the perfect way to start our married life.

During the next four years of our marriage, Doug and I went on many adventures. Sometimes we went alone, but mostly we brought Zach and Carter with us. We went on mountain bike trips to Moab in Utah, hiking trips to Sedona and backpacking trips to various places in the Rocky Mountains. Our favourite vacation with the boys was our trip to the Oregon Coast. We skimboarded with Zach and Carter for hours at Cannon Beach, a small beach town on the ocean. As the waves rolled out, we threw our thin, wooden boards down onto a skiff of water on the sand and then ran and jumped onto the boards, gliding down the beach for as long as we could. By the end of the day, all of us were covered in scrapes and bruises. It took us a long time to get the hang of it, but once we did, it became a much-loved pastime. Our campsite of choice was Honeyman State Park, which is only a short distance from Florence, Oregon. Honeyman Park is famous for its sand dunes. We loved running down the dunes as fast as we could straight into Cleawox Lake, laughing, splashing, and dunking one another. The lake was a perfect place to wash off the sandy grime. Our family loved the thrill of speed, so one day we rented sandboards, strapped them onto our feet as you would a snowboard, and then rode down the dunes. All day long, we hiked the dunes and found perfect lines to board down.

Another cherished holiday was our time hiking and camping at Lake O'Hara in Yoho National Park in the Canadian Rockies. Since my boys were babies, I had taken them to Lake O'Hara. I loved the unadulterated beauty of the place. Our early adventures often had fun mixed in with a whole pile of chaos. On one of our trips, in August 1999, when Carter was six months old and Zach two, the temperature surprisingly dropped to minus ten degrees Celsius. Carter was still been nursing and neither of the boys was potty trained. During the nights, we almost froze to death in our tent. Getting ready in the morning was a detailed, effortful production. After putting on multiple layers of warm clothing, without fail, Zach and Carter would poop their pants at the same time, setting us back hours. Sometimes, the effort outweighed the joy. In spite of the glitches, Lake O'Hara still held special meaning for me. When Doug and I planned to go with the boys in August 2008, it took me back to their earlier baby and toddler years, when they would marvel over sticks, bugs, and little holes in the dirt. I looked through old photo albums of our previous trips and was excited to go back now that they were older. Before leaving, Doug and I decided we wanted to be in complete comfort. We wanted a big tent where we would not be squished in like sardines. We wanted blow-up mattresses and a big stove to cook pancakes and bacon on in the morning. We were planning to camp in luxury. When we arrived at the parking lot, where the bus would transport our gear to our campsite, we were told we had to downsize. Lake O'Hara staff would not take our totes on the bus, so other campers had to lend us their bags to put our stuff in. The boys put layers of clothing on to free up some space in our bags and we ended up leaving a lot of our gear at the car. Those around us thought we had lost our minds. The commotion was embarrassing. Finally, after holding up the bus for far too long, we piled in. Partway up, our automatic air pump went off in one of our bags. Everyone on the bus stared at the Goodman comedy act. When we set up our over-sized tent, it hardly fit into the site. It looked like the Taj Mahal. A little kid walked past our tent and acted like she had seen the eighth wonder of the world, exclaiming "Daddy, look at their HUGE tent!" After two days, our luxurious mattresses had holes in them, leaving us sleeping on pieces of fabric. Nevertheless, we had a wonderful time of sharing and hiking familiar trails of the past.

We delighted in these fun-packed holidays, and even went on a few trips to Disneyland and the Dominican Republic. In between holidaying, I had the opportunity to go back to school and take a program through the Kelowna College of Professional Counsellors, which would eventually lead to obtaining a Master's Degree in counselling. For a pocket of time, we enjoyed our newly formed family without the constant presence of sorrow. We even had another wedding in our family when Ryan married Darcie's best friend Kirsten. For four years, God poured joy back into our hearts, and our lives were uninterrupted by tragedy.

Me with my beloved boys

Our 2008 trip to Lake O'Hara

Doug and his boys

Save me, O God, for the floodwaters are up to my neck.

Deeper and deeper I sink into the mire; I can't find a foothold.

I am in deep water, and the floods overwhelm me.

I am exhausted from crying for help; my throat is parched.

My eyes are swollen with weeping, waiting for my God to help me.

—Psalm 69:1-3 (NCV)

CHAPTER 4

LAND MINES

"How long must I tromp through this dense jungle half crazed and blind before the clearing appears?"

—Tilden H. Edward

Our four-year respite from heart pain sadly ended when Jay's mom was diagnosed with sarcoma in the winter of 2009. Sarcomas are quite rare in humans and tend to be the more lethal types of cancers. This news devastated our family. It had not even occurred to us that we would ever have to face cancer again, and yet, here we were faced with another terminal diagnosis. I was overwhelmed with life's cruel twists and turns.

Shortly after Maureen's diagnosis, we were blindsided by another unexpected turn of events. I woke up on the morning of June 24th, 2009, and got ready for a luncheon to honour teachers for their dedication and hard work. For the past three months, I had been filling in for a teacher on stress leave, teaching science and Bible at the Kamloops Christian School.

Even though I was excited for the luncheon, I felt heavy with thoughts of worry. For the past two weeks, Zach had been having unbearable head-aches, and experiencing double vision, nausea, and vomiting. His symp-toms were unsettling to say the least. One night we had found him lying on the floor beside his bed, and we could not wake him. He was a deep sleeper so we did not think too much about it at the time. But his head-aches were relentless and very worrying. We had taken Zach to the Royal Inland Hospital emergency room three times in one week and the nurses kept sending us home. We made appointments with massage therapists, thinking that school stress must be causing tension and pain. Zach's doctor explained that twelve-year-olds sometimes get these symptoms due to hormones, but my intuition told me something was seriously wrong. It gnawed at me day and night. On top of worrying about Zach's health, I was also worried about Doug. He had developed a lump on the side of his neck. My mother-in-law and I had recently gone for lunch, and I had mentioned to her my tendency to catastrophize everything. In my imagination, I had already played out my worst nightmare: they both had tumours. As it turned out, they did.

I had just finished blow-drying my hair and putting on my makeup when Carter came into my room and said, "Mom, Zach's acting really weird." He told me how Zach had been playing video games down-stairs and all of a sudden he had become disoriented and confused. When I came into the room, Zach was slurring his speech, and I felt terror course through my body. Something was horribly wrong. A little later, he had trouble getting dressed because he could not coordinate his limbs to do what he wanted them to do. He could not even get his flip-flops on. Memories of Jay's diagnosis exploded in my mind. *God, please don't let this happen again! I can't do this twice.* Frantically, I drove Zach to the Urgent Care Walk-in Clinic, but due to the severity of his symp-toms, the lady at the front desk advised us to go directly to the ER. Zach screamed in agony in the waiting room of the ER, his eyes wild with fear.

Nobody would be sending us home this time. Waves of hysteria pushed against me. Hospital staff admitted Zach immediately. By then, he was not making any sense at all. He could not speak properly and he seemed frantically confused. The doctor examining him seemed frustrated with Zach's inability to comprehend or tell him the origin of his pain. Zach stared at him, mumbling indecipherable words. The doctor ordered a CT scan and gave him a shot to calm him down. Everything was in agonizingly slow motion as nurses placed him into the CT scanner. An all-too-familiar darkness enveloped me. Worst-case scenarios flooded my mind as we waited for the doctor's report.

Mercifully, after the CT scan Zach slept peacefully, and I was so thankful he was not in misery for the time being. As the doctor pulled back the curtain, I saw "the look" in his eyes—he was about to deliver bad news. "I am sorry," he said. "We were not expecting this. Your son has a mass in his brain that is the size of a nectarine. We are going to need to intubate him and fly him immediately to Children's Hospital in Vancouver." What I was hearing was too much to take in. My sweet Zach, so vibrant and so young, lay innocently in front of me as I tried to absorb what I was hearing. When he had been a little boy, I had rocked him and read him *Love You Forever* by Robert Munsch, memorizing his features and how he felt and smelled. I had relished that time of being able to keep him safe from harm. For some reason though, even then, I had sensed I may not have him forever. Now, as the news began to settle, I felt helpless to save my baby. There is no feeling to describe the physical and emotional pain of hearing news that crushes every dream you have ever had. Hope dies in a split second, and all that remains is unyielding pain.

Doctors, anesthetists, and nurses prepared Zach for transport. Tubes were coming from every direction, IV poles were attached, and phone calls were made to Vancouver to prepare for his arrival. People frantically worked to get him ready to go. I had finally gotten in touch with

Doug, and he was driving the car to meet Zach and I in Vancouver. Plans were made for Carter to stay with my mom and Ray. The medical team transported Zach and I out to the plane. All the way to Vancouver, I listened to him breathing in and out, not fully connected to what was happening. I was numb and in horrific pain all at the same time. As soon as we arrived at Children's Hospital, nurses rushed Zach inside to have an MRI. Dr. Cochrane, Zach's neurosurgeon, came in shortly after with the scan and showed Doug and I the mass on Zach's brain. He was hopeful it might be something other than a tumour, but he needed to do a craniotomy to be sure. A craniotomy involves the surgical removal of part of the bone from the skull to expose the brain. Tools are used to temporarily remove a section of bone called the bone flap, which is replaced after brain surgery has been performed. The thought of this procedure happening to my boy terrified me.

Ryan and Kirsten soon arrived with care packages. We updated them on what was happening, and emotions surged through all of us: fear of the unknown, dread about what tomorrow could bring and helplessness at not being able to change anything. Thinking back, I am not sure why we did not huddle together and pray right then. Maybe we were too weary or shell-shocked or sad to voice our thoughts to God. For me, I think shock had taken over any rational thinking. I wrestled just to draw a breath. Even though the gravity of the situation trumped smaller emotions like reassurance, I still felt lifted up by Ryan and Kirsten's presence. I was thankful they were standing in the hurt alongside us. I wished Carter could be with us. I missed him, and I desperately, protectively, wanted him near me. It hurt my heart to think about what he must be going through back home. I also craved my mom's comfort.

Doug and I lay down on the floor of a tiny waiting room that night and, strangely, we actually slept. When I awoke in the morning, I was uneasy and disoriented. A terrible ache rushed into my heart as I remembered where we were and why we were in this strange room. Fear caught in my throat. I wondered how many other families had slept in this room, waiting to hear news about their child. The word "cancer" pounded like a drumbeat in my head, relentless and obsessive. *Cancer. Cancer. Cancer.* Dr. Cochrane came to tell us that the mass was a tumour, but that we would have to wait to find out the type and prognosis. All of a sudden, I had to get to Zach immediately, as if I had to rescue him out of a burning building. I did not want him to feel scared and alone. We were allowed to visit him, and what I saw when I got into the ICU room broke my heart in a way I never thought possible. He looked so helpless and alone. His head was bandaged and his eyes were swollen. He still looked like Zach, but not the Zach I knew. He looked weary and wounded. We waited anxiously by his bed for him to wake up. I would not leave Zach's side for even a small break because I could not handle the thought of him waking up with machines, webs of intravenous lines, and strangers all around him. The room felt cold and institutional. Each bed in the room had a critically ill child surrounded by machines and devices. Scores of hospital staff monitored each child's care around the clock, checking vitals and administering pain medication. As I looked around, I wondered if the other families' bad news was as bad as ours. Doug and I still felt too numb to pray. In those moments, God felt like a stone statue, incapable or unwilling to help us when we needed it most. Steeped in pain, it was impossible to see anything but the darkness that surrounded us. Never in my life had God seemed so puny, powerless and distant.

When Zach awoke, his beautiful brown eyes were full of fear. Usually, his eyes would dance with life, full of imagination, wonder, and laughter. The eyes staring back at me now made me feel like someone had taken a dagger and jabbed it straight into my heart. Zach had no idea where he was or what had happened to him. I reassured him, telling him he had gone through an operation to get rid of the pain in his head. He looked so small and vulnerable. Later, Zach fell back to sleep with his hand tucked under his cheek, just as he had done as a baby. I sat listening to the whirring of machines around Zach and anger, sadness, confusion, and anxiety collided inside of me. Cancer was ravaging my boy, and I was helpless to do anything about it. God felt worse than a bully. He felt like the one who watches bullying and does nothing to intervene. I related to C. S. Lewis who, during a night season of grief declared: "Go to [God] when your need is desperate, when all other help is vain and what do you find? A door slammed in your face, and a sound of bolting and double bolting on the other side. After that, silence."[1] God's silence in my present state of fear left me feeling utterly forsaken. Hope vanished and light ceased to exist.

You keep track of all my sorrows.
You have collected all my tears in your bottle.
You have recorded each one in your book.

Psalm 56:8 (NLT)

CHAPTER 5

TEAR SOUP

"Grandy's arms ached and she felt stone cold and empty. There were no words that could describe the pain she was feeling. What's more, when she looked out the window it surprised her to see how the rest of the world was going on as usual while her world had stopped."

— *Tear Soup* by Pat Schwiebert and Chuck Deklyen

Chronic heartache and disappointment filled our nightmarish week at Children's Hospital. When we thought it could not get any worse, we received a phone call from Kamloops confirming Doug had a cancerous tumour on his neck called squamous cell carcinoma. Everything became a blur and the fog filling my head refused to clear. We had meetings and MRI's, and spent late nights in fetal positions on the couch in Zach's hospital room, trying to absorb our new reality. I had to handle this somehow. My husband and my son would be doing radiation and chemotherapy together, and Carter also needed my support and love to navigate through this horror. I shuffled down the hospital corridors willing one foot to step in front of the other. I had once read that sighing is a sign of grief. It felt like all I did during those hospital days was sigh. I had to command my body to move. *Get out of bed. Get in the shower. Put soap in your hair.* People talked to me, but I could not make sense of their words. I had to remind myself to blink because I knew my blank stare and hollow eyes must have been making people feel awkward. Sometimes, I would find myself laughing, conversing, and taking part in activities, but I was not present. I lived in my head, separated from the messiness of my heart. To keep from going insane I had to anesthetize my heart in order to function. Counselors call this denial. I called it survival. It was not a conscious decision, but I was aware I felt more like a block of cement than a human being.

In the middle of it all, though, traces of grace surfaced in my thoughts. I was reminded of a story a friend told Jay and I during our darkest times, a gentle reminder of how God covers us when life throws unrelenting blows. In this story, a fire rips through a farm and destroys everything in its path. The next morning the farmer walks across the yard and stops as he almost steps on the charred body of a hen. He moves it gently with his boot, and there underneath are her chicks, all of them still alive. She had gathered them under her wings and placed her body between them and the flames. God helped me connect this story to a verse Zach had underlined as his own special verse in the Bible: "When you go through deep waters and great trouble, I will be with you. When you go through rivers of difficulty, you will not drown! When you walk through the fire of oppression, you will not be burned up; the flames will not consume you. For I am the Lord, your God" (Isaiah 43:2). Even as cancer raged around us, Jesus gathered our family under his wings and buffered us. A pilot light of hope trickled in to my heart. An inkling of faith helped me keep breathing. Just when I thought I could not take one more step, God drew me in and sheltered me. I sensed his love. But, too soon after these moments I would buckle under grief again, pleading, kicking, and screaming at God, echoing David in the Psalms and Jesus on the cross, "Why have you forsaken me?" (Psalm 22:1)

My three dear friends from Gold River, Cheryl, Kate, and Corrine, arrived at the hospital on June 26th a few days after they had found out about Zach. When I saw them I felt great relief. During Jay's sickness, they had been with me, letting me rant and rave, and helping me laugh when I no longer thought it was possible. They had prayed with me, encouraged me to talk, and just let me sit in silence. I loved them so much, and having them there with me again was like having shock absorbers for all that was coming up against us. They always knew what to say and when to say it. I cannot remember what Corrine said when she first saw me, but soon the three of us broke out laughing and could not stop. Immediately after the laughing fit, we all burst into tears. My friends were my ministering angels during these dark days.

Although Zach's biopsy results still had not come in, the surgeons were pleased with how he was recovering from surgery. His sense of humour was returning, and he did not seem to have any cognitive deficits from the craniotomy. Kirsten regularly checked in on Zach during her breaks. She worked in labour and delivery at BC Women's Hospital, in the same building as BC Children's Hospital. One evening Doug and I stepped out for dinner, and when we walked back into Zach's room we were met with uproarious laughter. Kirsten and Zach were watching his favourite movie, *Nacho Libre* with Jack Black. Zach's eyes were still swollen shut from surgery so he could only hear the movie. He would listen for his favourite lines and then both he and Kirsten would erupt into giggles. They anticipated the part in the movie when the character Natcho says to his friend, Chanco, "When you are a man, sometimes you wear stretchy pants in your room. It's for fun." At this point laughter broke out, the DVD would be rewound and they would listen to it again, laughing just as hard as the first time. I stood in the doorway, amazed at how all that had come at Zach over the past five days could not steal his joy.

Six days after he was admitted, Zach was released to go home. We had hoped to get the pathology report before leaving the hospital, but the results had still not come in. A pathology report is a document that contains the diagnosis determined by examining cells and tissues under a microscope. Dr. Cochrane met with us and assured us the results would be in within the next few days. Being out of the hospital felt so good, but it also reminded me of the enormity of our trauma. Other people were carrying on with life, buying groceries, driving kids to soccer, going to work, and playing at the park. Meanwhile, our lives had come to a screeching halt. I realized other people's joy actually brought me pain. Now, the waiting game at home would begin, where we would sit agonizingly by the phone for the call to come that would determine whether my son had a curable or terminal cancer. The days ahead terrified me. Fortunately, the thought of connecting again with Carter bolstered my spirits significantly. I knew his loving, funny ways would be so refreshing. I craved his laughter and light-heartedness, reminders that normal still existed. When we arrived home, I could see the past week had taken its toll on Carter. He evaded eye contact, trying to bypass what might be revealed if he were to look into our hearts. He did not ask a lot of questions about his brother, but rather talked incessantly about irrelevant topics, hoping to delay hearing news that would shatter his heart. He wanted to go back to the way things had been only one week before, but Zach was tired and dismissive. I tried to talk with Carter, but he would put up a wall of protection. He was not ready to hear the painful truth.

That night, after the boys were tucked into bed, I went down to the computer to research childhood brain tumours. I felt peace wash over me because, for the most part, children Zach's age typically had good outcomes. I breathed a sigh of relief. Most likely surgeons would be able to operate and remove the tumour. Then we could go back to living our lives. I talked myself into believing the results of the biopsy would be good news and went to bed and slept in peace.

The day the phone call came in from BC Children's Hospital, Carter and Doug were not home. I had been burdened with worry for Carter, so Doug had taken him for a little getaway to Vancouver to see Ryan and Darcie. I could tell Carter needed a break from all the sudden changes. He had become saturated with fear about what was going to happen next. He did not verbalize his fear, but his pain showed in his body language. He needed a break from the complex, confusing emotions swirling around him. He could escape the heaviness of our home for a little while. I watched Zach tinker with his Legos, oblivious, for the moment, of all he had endured over the past week. The phone rang, and when I picked up, I recognized Dr. Cochrane's voice instantly. My heart went into an irregular rhythm as I went out into the garden to talk with him. He told me the results had come in and Zach had a very rare and aggressive tumour called glioblastoma multiforme. He thought the most time Zach had left was one year. One year! I was beyond tears. My heart hurt and my head throbbed. I wanted to scream, but words did not come. Instead, I sat in stunned silence. Slowly, after putting down the phone, the nauseating realization that I had to go back in the house to share this news with my son dawned on me. *How does a mom break such horrific news to her child?* I felt light headed and sick. Instinctively, I wanted to buffer Zach, but he needed to know the truth. I could not hide and act as though this dreadful reality did not exist. I knew the silence would scare him even more than my words. I braced myself for the hardest thing I have ever had to do in my life.

I went into the house and just stared at him while he played with his Legos, aware that he was still excited to be missing school and thrilled to have endless hours to make his creations. I realized it was the last time I would see him play this freely, without the fear of cancer looming over him. He looked up at me with his innocent eyes and asked, "Who was on the phone, Mom?"

"It was Dr. Cochrane, Zach."

"What does he want?"

"He wanted to share the results of the tests that came back about why you have been having such severe headaches."

"What did he say?"

I lowered myself to the floor, and then the tears came.

"Honey, you have a brain tumour."

"Is it cancer?"

"Yes it is."

"Am I going to die?"

"The doctors are doing everything they can to find a way to treat this, but yes, there is a possibility you may die."

He looked up at me in terror and all I could do was hold him. "Zach, let's pray that God will give you the courage to face this and that he will take away your fear." We prayed together, cried together, and just sat together in silence. He called his Grandma Laird and wailed into the phone, "Grandma, I have cancer!" She soothed him with her love and gentleness, and he got off the phone a lot calmer.

"Mom, when am I going to die?" Time stood still as I choked the words out.

"The doctor said you have one year, maybe more."

He was quiet for a minute and then looked up at me with pain, but also hope. "Oh, so I have a whole year?" His comment baffled me. To him, a year was a lifetime. He went back to playing with his Legos, thankful he had an entire year. I was astonished. Only God could have given him such supernatural peace.

Unlike Zach, I had no peace. A cesspool of anger churned inside of me. I silently scream at God, *I am not planning this child's funeral! He is only twelve years old. He has his whole life ahead of him. Surely this is not OK with you!* I felt immobilized, stuck in quicksand and unable to stop the train wreck that loomed around the corner. I paced back and forth waiting for Doug and Carter to get home from Vancouver, trying to put a lid on the frantic feelings ripping and tearing the inside of me. When I heard the car pull into the driveway, I had to resist the urge to run and hide. Bone tired, I made my way to the garage and shut the door behind me. I intercepted Doug and Carter before they came into the house, wanting to cushion them from the blow. "Dr. Cochrane phoned three hours ago," I said numbly. "The news is not good. We need to have a family meeting when we get inside." I sounded a lot calmer than I felt. Summoning a family meeting was my last memory until I put the boys to bed that night. What we talked about is still buried in layers of grief. I tucked Zach and Carter into bed around 9 pm. Terrified of the dark thoughts that might be circling in Zach's head, I gave him some melatonin. I prayed sleep would give him respite from fear.

On a rare day shortly thereafter, when I was able to push back debilitating sadness, I found an old journal entry between God and I that I had recorded before Zach and Doug had been diagnosed. In it, I shared with God how I had a sense my children were in danger. Doug and I had been in Jamaica in December 2008, and while we were there, I had not been able to shake a foreboding sense that something was not right. On the way home on the plane, I had silently prayed, *God, do not ever let anything awful happen to my children. I would not survive.* As I shared my uneasy feelings with God, he had assured me he loved my children even more than I did and he was summoning angels to fight on our behalf. God had known long before I had what was coming my way. He had promised me beforehand that heaven's armies would be released to help us endure the hard days ahead.

Although God's promise to send angelic help gave me strength, his reassurance faded in the days ahead as the ground gave way underneath me, day after endless day. I often found myself whirling completely out of control. The only reason I kept returning to God was because I knew I could not do it on my own. His comfort and love seemed like fantasy in this valley, but the risk of living without him was too high. Without God, this kind of pain would only lead to death. Remembering Jesus was not immune to suffering did keep a pinprick of faith alive, protecting me from giving up on God altogether. Jesus had been where I was. In his own body, he had experienced our family's gut-wrenching emotions. He hurt, bled, cried and suffered alongside us. I related the psalmist David when he wrote about how his strength had dried up "like sun baked clay" (Psalm 22:15). I could not see my way through the valley, but I sensed, somehow, Jesus would make a way for us through the dark, desert land — this I chose to believe. I had recently read Women of Faith speaker Nicole Johnson's book, *Stepping into the Ring,* and I tucked her promises close to my heart:

"No one who fights with their hope in the Lord ever loses the last round. Today is only one chapter, not the complete book of your life. You may have cancer, but cancer does not have you. Cancer can take your cells, but it cannot take you. Cancer can have your hair, but it cannot have your heart. When the last bell rings, cancer may stand in the center alone, but it will not be the winner. In order for cancer to win, it would have to be able to follow you beyond the grave, and it cannot. It will be left alone in the ring with a tired, worn-out shell. Your life will be with the One in whom you have put your hope, the author of everlasting life."[1]

Fighting back ever-present tears and the urge to give up, I continually fought hard to keep bringing myself back to God's promises, such as these. I knew no matter how ugly the journey got, all would be well in the end. In the present, however, there were no words to fully console my heart.

During this time of trying to cope, I never really knew how I felt about anything. It was as if someone had taken my feelings, put them into a blender, and scrambled them all up, making it impossible for me to decipher between one feeling and another. Did I love God or hate him? Did I resent him? Did I believe in him? Was he my all-in-all? I had talked to people about his love and his goodness navigating us through this storm, but did I really believe it? Confusion distorted everything and life was like trying to walk through a terrifying maze with no sense of direction.

I'll never forget the trouble, the utter lostness, the taste of ashes, the poison I've swallowed. I remember it all — oh, how well I remember — the feeling of hitting the bottom.

Lamentations 3:19-20 (MSG)

CHAPTER 6

MAYHEM

"In the middle of the journey of our life I found myself within a dark woods where the straight way was lost."

—Dante Alighieri

The days and weeks following Zach's diagnosis were a blur of decisions and unfathomable upheaval. I could feel my heart beating, but I was dead inside. Groceries had to be bought, Carter needed to get to school, phone calls needed to be made, and life had to continue. We became the family others would refer to when they were having a bad day. I could imagine people saying, "Life could be worse; we could be going through what the Goodmans are going through." I could not imagine ever feeling happiness again. I knew God promised to be close to those with broken hearts, but those words seemed like lies. The appalling injustice unfolding in our lives seemed to go unnoticed by God. I had to rely on what my head was telling me and not my heart. My head reminded me of God's promise never to leave us, but my heart screamed otherwise.

Faith became a daily choice. Choosing faith felt robotic and empty, but my shambled emotions were a poor alternative as a compass. My heart would have led me into dangerous places of unbelief. True to my pattern of coping, I went on autopilot so I could make life-altering decisions about my family's care. I had heard of mothers becoming so depressed during similar crises they shut down completely. In a comatose state, they would become incapable of caring for their own needs or their family's needs. I wanted that luxury. I wished for a reason not to get up in the morning. It was costly to keep functioning, but I had no choice.

The loathsome intruder in Doug's and Zach's bodies had me brooding about our future. *What hope do we have?* Mechanically, I began to ponder the next step we needed to take. We had to decide where Doug and Zach were going to have their treatments. As they would be doing radiation at the same time, it made sense for both of them to have their treatments in Kelowna. This meant Zach would not be at BC Children's Hospital with other children going through similar experiences. I felt sad because Vancouver is equipped with child therapists and programs to help kids find joy and strength in the midst of treatment. But at least we could all be together this way. Doubts about putting Zach through the brutal process of chemotherapy and radiation began to trouble me. *With a dismal one percent chance of survival, what is the logic behind chemotherapy? If we do not go through with the treatment, will I be OK with my decision? Is this even my decision? What does Zach want? He has to be a part of the decision because he has the right to choose how he wants to live his life, but is it fair to place this responsibility on a twelve-year-old child?* Normally prayer would be the only way to make a choice of this magnitude, but lately God had not proven to be too reliable. I did not feel like praying, and when I did, it was forced and unnatural. Distraught over his own diagnosis, Doug could not carry these burdensome decisions on his shoulders. I felt utterly alone and responsible for carrying the heaviness on my own.

In the middle of July 2009, we met with the oncologist in Kelowna to discuss Doug and Zach's treatment protocol. Jolts of emotions warred within me as she described her recommendations for Zach. I felt physically ill. As she talked about the side effects of chemotherapy and radiation, I realized we had grossly underestimated the intensity of the treatments. I shared how unsettled I was about following through with the doctor's recommendations. I had watched Jay go through treatments and did not want the same trauma for Zach—the vomiting, trauma, thrush (yeast infections of the mouth caused by a compromised immune system), low energy, depression, anxiety, fear, and hospital stays. All of it seemed too high a cost for an incurable cancer. I wanted his last days spent out in the sun, climbing trees, with beauty around him, enjoying his friends and family. Her response to my concerns insinuated that refusing treatment would be the equivalent of neglect. Looking back on it later, I realized I had felt coerced into going through with treatment, against my own good judgment. It was a decision I still regret.

After our meeting with the oncologist about Zach, we met with the same oncologist about Doug. We knew Doug had cancer, but were blindsided when we learned he had a stage three cancer. Stage three means it is a larger cancer and has spread into the surrounding tissues and lymph nodes. He required three rounds of chemotherapy along with thirty-seven radiation treatments. His particular chemotherapy, Cisplatin, was one of the more toxic kinds, causing violent vomiting, weight loss, hearing loss and risk of damage to the heart and kidneys. Radiation would leave him with severely impaired saliva glands, meaning he could have a dry mouth for the rest of his life. Burns from treatment would leave open, raw wounds, likely resulting in the installation of a feeding tube because swallowing would be too painful. Our lives, in that moment, felt like someone had taken a wrecking ball and smashed us to smithereens.

Within the next hour, I knew Zach needed to have his radiation mask fitted, but I could not imagine making it through even the next minute.

The thought of the hours, days, and weeks ahead plummeted me into despair. My pain reached a zenith when they placed Zach on a metal bed and put hot gauze over his face to harden and form a mold. Radiotherapy has to be aimed very precisely, so a mask needed to be made to hold his head in place because any movement could change the area that got treated, with catastrophic results. Once the mask is fitted, it is fixed to the radiation treatment table to ensure the head is held in exactly the right position. When I saw him lying on the table, pinned down and helpless, I felt like someone had their hands around my neck, choking the life out of me. Zach looked afraid and vulnerable. If this had been in a dream, I would have woken up at this moment and realized it was all a horrible nightmare. But this was real. On the way home, we sat in silence, each of us trying to process our own fears. As usual Zach talked, seemingly unfazed by what had just happened. Denying the severity of his situation was his way of coping. I longed for solitude. I ached to escape from the pain of our lives. I could not imagine anything getting better and the hopelessness felt unbearable. I wanted to be alone to grieve loudly and let the pain go without worrying I would upset others.

Soon after we got home from Kelowna, we had a meeting with a pediatrician in Kamloops, Dr. Trent Smith, who explained the details of Zach's chemotherapy treatments. It would be taken orally in a pill form for five consecutive days, every twenty-eight days. One hour before his dose, he would take an antiemetic to control nausea and vomiting. On July 27th, 2009, I started giving Zach Temozolomide, along with Ondansetrone for nausea. If doctors had been administering these drugs, I would have felt less overwhelmed, because when I was giving them to him, I felt somehow responsible for his suffering. It felt counterintuitive for a mother to give her child a drug that would make him sick and cause his body to become weak and tired.

We began to look for accommodations in Kelowna. We did not want to stay in a hotel during treatments. We wanted to be in a place that was a home away from home. Margie knew people who had a condo up at Big White, so we arranged to stay there. Thankfully, due to summer break, Carter would be able to join us. At the end of July, with anxiety pushing hard against us, we piled into our minivan, Kelowna-bound, to begin Doug and Zach's radiation treatments. The trip felt like the end of everything good that had ever existed in our lives. I pondered past summers of camping, fishing, going to the Oregon Coast, enjoying sunny days at Shuswap Lake, and getting ice cream on hot days. What now? It was impossible to imagine a future without suffering. It did not look like there would ever be a happy ending; there was no finish line for the path we were on. When we arrived at Big White, I was thankful to be in nature and away from the city and the chaos. Maybe here we could find some rest. We put our groceries away and settled into our new home. For a while, we could pretend we were here on a holiday, sharing time together, and enjoying a family vacation. We could fantasize that cancer was not our new reality. I could forget, even if it was only for a little while, that I might have to live the rest of my life without my precious Zach.

The sun enticed us out for a walk in the later afternoon. We found fresh huckleberries on a little trail that meandered through the forest, a trail we would venture down often. The sun felt warm and life giving, the opposite environment of my inner state. I chose to savour these moments with my family. When I looked at Zach, though, I could tell putting one foot in front of the other was exhausting him, and this knowledge shattered my heart. And although Doug participated in body, his fear held him in an emotionally dark and distant place. I tried to be light-hearted to counteract the heavy atmosphere, but my effort felt draining. Whatever we did today, the next day could not be avoided.

In the morning, the four of us journeyed down the hill for Doug and Zach's appointment. As we got closer to the hospital, my sadness deepened. Objects around me were blurred as I stared into space. In spite of increasing heaviness, I tried to keep the conversation light. Zach interrupted my small talk, "Stop! I'm going to be sick." We pulled over quickly as Zach threw up out the window. The chemotherapy had started taking effect and his body was responding to the assault. I hugged him, barely able to stand under the crushing sorrow. *This is only the beginning,* I thought to myself. I broke off a piece of a yellow anti-nausea pill and he slipped it under his tongue. Somehow, sadness felt too vulnerable right then. Anger felt more powerful and efficient. I could still get things done when I was angry, whereas sadness just threatened to incapacitate me. Anger tricked me into believing I could fight cancer with adrenalin, masking the intensity of my pain enough so I could still function day to day. I hesitated before stepping out of the van. I did not want to step foot into the hospital. I desperately wanted to avoid the inevitable.

Our footsteps echoed down the hallway as the four of us trudged to the radiation rooms. Trauma heightened my senses. The slightest smell was pungent and nauseating. Lights made my eyes hurt and my vision become blurry. Even the sounds of our own footsteps agitated me. I felt like I was going crazy. *Why do people need to be so loud,* I wondered. All I could hear was chaos banging around in my head. We passed a fish tank with a disfigured fish swimming awkwardly in its cramped tank. *Figures,* I thought, *even the fish are damaged.* After seemingly endless hallways, we arrived at the radiation room. Each room had a different name: The Park, The Orchard, The Beach, The Lake, The Hills and The Cabin. It was almost laughable. Obviously, the person who had named these rooms had never gone through what we were going through. I could think of more fitting names. I appreciated the efforts to make this place of brokenness palatable, but it would take more than comfort names to do that. Zach settled into a chair in the waiting room, made small talk with a few people and picked up a Reader's Digest. Doug mindlessly leafed through a magazine and Carter and I just stared blankly at nothing. I glanced at the others in the room. A few worked on a puzzle in the middle of the table, seemingly unfazed by their diagnosis. *Do I look as normal as they do?*

I asked myself. Had they not been in "The Orchard" room, I would not have known their lives had been shattered by cancer. *How can they still their whirring minds long enough to fit pieces of a puzzle together?* I could feel my jaw clenching and my chest constricting. Unlike the others in this room, I could not hide the intensity of my anguish. I had trouble sitting still. Brooding left untamed energy heaving in my body. I just wanted to go for a run to get rid of it. I could understand why animals pace when they are stressed. I felt compelled to move, and sitting still with my thoughts felt like torture. Finally, Doug and Zach were called. After only ten minutes they were finished. The radiologist took Zach to the calendar where he marked an x after each treatment. At the end of each week, he would receive a special gift as encouragement to keep going.

Over the next few days, the drive from Big White to the hospital and back became torturous, especially for Doug. He felt isolated and worried about staying so far from town and away from the hospital. His anxiety became debilitating. Smells bothered him and he felt generally unable to cope. The chemotherapy treatments poisoned him, not just physically, but also emotionally, psychologically, and spiritually. The open sore radiation burns on his neck and on the inside of his throat became so raw he could not swallow food. To prevent the muscles in his throat from atrophying, I would cut up cucumber for him to swallow, but even swallowing a little amount of food became impossible. He started to lose massive amounts of weight, until finally the oncologist ordered a feeding tube. I could not tolerate the thought of pouring Boost down his feeding tube, so I began making my own highly nutritious cocktails to give him. However, that too ended up being a gong show, because without fail, the tube would get clogged, Doug would get frustrated, and I would feel like admitting myself into the psychiatric ward.

The intensity of Doug's cancer symptoms trapped him in his own world of pain, frustration and fear. He wished he could isolate himself from our family and deal with his cancer alone. His world of chaos made it impossible for him to be in tune with our needs. Being with us only reminded him of the ways he was letting us down. Watching his family suffer and helpless to do anything about it riddled him with guilt. Increasingly weighed down with all he could not be for us, he retreated into his own world. The more he withdrew from family life, the lonelier I got. I found it difficult to talk with Doug because he was part of my trauma, and Doug found it challenging to talk with me because grief clouded my ability to take in his painful emotions. I felt incompetent on so many levels. Doug sensed the anger and resentment I tried to hide, but both of us knew delving into our feelings would be like setting a match to gasoline. Instead, we both internalized the pain of our inner worlds. Infected with grief, we found it difficult to relate to each other and to those around us. On days when being a caregiver felt particularly hard, people would ask how I was doing. I would say the usual "I'm OK" or "I'm hanging in there." A more honest answer would have been "I feel like I'm being suffocated, and my life isn't mine anymore, and I really wish I could run away." The pain felt beyond endurance. I wanted to savour my moments with Zach, knowing time was not on our side, yet I could not give him my undivided attention. I did not have time to steep in memory making and this hurt my heart more than anything. I could not love enough, support enough, care enough, or be fun enough. I was dying inside and yet I thought I had to be the sponge to soak up my family's fear, pain, and loss.

Our family needed professional help, but Doug and I did not have the energy for counselling. We set up appointments for Zach and Carter instead. I booked an appointment with a child therapist from the cancer clinic. During Zach and Carter's first visit, she read them *Corey, the Coping Caterpillar*, a book about grief designed for five-year-olds. Zach was almost thirteen, and Carter would rather slam his head into a wall than see a counselor, so being treated like five-year-olds offended them. From that day forward, they would duck behind the plants and hide from the therapist if they saw her in the hallway. Doug and I laughed and promised them we would not make them go back. I tried one more time to get Carter to see a counsellor and beforehand he assured me that if I sent him, he would just sit there. Apparently, at the next appointment that is exactly what he did. Our help from professional counsellors had seemed futile.

Fortunately, our help from family members and friends remained consistent. Knowing how drained I was, Margie came to stay with us at Big White to relieve our burdens. She instinctively knew what we needed, so I did not feel like I needed to entertain her or help her figure out how to navigate our world. She simply jumped on board and did what needed to be done, whether that meant vacuuming, making a meal, administering pain medication, or being comic relief for the kids. She got into the rhythm of the chaos and lifted some of our weariness. When she would leave to go back to her home in Canmore, I would feel crushing heaviness return. Every two weeks, Margie would make the journey from Canmore to care for us and I would count down the days from when she left until she came back.

On Fridays, as soon as radiation was done, we would go back to Kamloops for the weekend and settle into a slower, more relaxed pace, free from the downpour of chaos. However, weekends had their unwanted surprises. The radiation had agitated Zach's tumour, and for whatever reason, the steroid typically given to reduce swelling had not been prescribed. On August 8th, 2009, Margie and I were in the kitchen cooking (and drinking wine, I am sure), when Zach came out of the TV room struggling to walk, disoriented and slurring his words. Doug stayed with Carter while Margie and I rushed Zach to the hospital. We told the doctors about his history and our suspicion that he needed Decadron to bring down the swelling, but because Coastal Health and Interior Health are not connected, Kamloops doctors could not access Zach's file from Vancouver. Eventually, they were able to connect the dots and started administering IV Decadron. The pediatrician suggested we go home and pack our things because Zach would likely be transported by air to Vancouver. I went home to pack my bags. On my way back to the hospital, I prayed God would intervene because Doug would not be able to manage on his own if we had to go to Vancouver. I made my way into the ER, peered around the curtain, and Zach said, "Hey, Mom, how's it going?" My cheerful boy seemed perfectly normal and the air transport had been cancelled. To be cautious, they admitted Zach overnight and released him the next day.

The Decadron did wonders for his energy and reduced all the swelling in his brain, so he had no physical or cognitive deficits. Over time, though, the steroid caused face swelling that made Zach self-conscious and became a wrenching reminder for me that something was wrong. His symptoms continually reminded me of what I was losing. Despite these physical reminders, I refused to believe Zach was dying. I started researching for hours on the Internet to find answers, determined to know everything about his disease. My panic-driven research became all encompassing. I read everything I could get my hands on. I wanted as much information as I could get, even though everything I read led to the same conclusion: my child was going to die in a very short period of time. The more I read, the guiltier I became. There are many opinions regarding the origins of cancer, from genetics or personality, to a negative outlook on life. *Have I instilled a negative self-image in Zach that has led to the development of cancer? Have I been too critical of him, too demanding? Has faulty parenting caused this?* Guilt consumed me like a disease. I felt deep regret over the times I had yelled and broken his sensitive heart. I thought of the many times I had pushed him too hard toward excellence, which may have made him feel he did not measure up. Memories flashed of homework nights ending in tears. I wanted a redo. I wanted to back up time so I could heal the areas in him I had bruised. I would do so much differently.

I felt like a lost soul when I pictured life without Zach and I was driven to find a way to stop his disease. I became the supplement hound, doling out vitamins, making disgusting juices, introducing a vegan diet, and generally, making life more impossible than it already was. I dedicated every ounce of my energy into stopping the inevitable future the doctors kept talking about. In spite of my efforts though, things kept getting worse. Abnormal stress caused abnormal ways of coping. Instinctively, I knew there needed to be a change in my approach, but gritty determination compelled me to continue, even if the costs outweighed the benefits. If I did not ask questions, take charge, and take responsibility, I feared depression and hopelessness would drag me into a pit from which I would never be able to escape. I decided to dig in and fight to the bitter end to save my child's life. Letting go meant giving up, so I continued with what I was doing, refusing to listen to anyone who insinuated I should lighten up. Rationally, I knew tumours as aggressive as Zach's were not impressed with chlorophyll, intravenous vitamin C, mistletoe injections, and massive amounts of supplements, but I could not bring myself to a place of peace about letting go. Seismic fear compelled me to keep searching for answers.

My compulsion tended to push others away. An obsessed person does not allow others to help because they cannot do it right, and sadly, I thought I was the only one capable of "doing it right." I controlled and micro-managed details of Doug's and Zach's care. Other family members felt tense around me because I would become agitated and irritable when they deviated from my plan. For example, one evening, Grandma and Grandpa Laird brought over one of Zach's favourite foods: white rice sushi. But, because of the white rice I would not allow Zach to eat it; as if white rice determined whether he lived or died! To me, nonconformity to the eating plan meant the tumours were thriving, and I wanted to do everything to shrink them. Tumours feed on sugar, so if Doug or Zach ate any sugary food, I would lose sleep at night. If they missed a round of vitamins, I felt like the tumours gained the upper hand. I could find no peace or rest, and neither could those close to me. Family and friends were gracious, though, and often made vegan meals, lovingly putting food in glass containers so toxins in the plastic would not release any harmful chemicals into the food. Their compassion moved them to go the extra mile for us.

My frenzied search for cures for Zach's cancer left me anxious and disappointed. I was terrified of making the wrong decision. I was uncertain about continuing on with chemotherapy, for fear of it increasing Zach' suffering. Striving to gain more time at the expense of quality time seemed cruel. When I asked Zach if he was scared, he said, "Yes, I'm afraid of the chemo." Puzzled, I questioned whether he feared the chemo more than the cancer. Without hesitation, he said the chemo scared him more. I did not know what to do with that information. It felt selfish to keep suggesting he do treatments when the treatments scared him more than the disease. "Zach, what do you want to do?" His fear of dying was at the forefront of his mind, so he decided to continue with treatment. This kind of lose-lose decision-making left me weary and confused. There seemed to be no resolution.

Throughout these painful days, my heart found it hard to be still long enough to talk with God. Whenever I tried to focus on God, I felt pressure mounting inside of me. I had to move to tame the wild, painful feelings. The sicker Doug and Zach became, the greater the chasm between God and I became. My focus on research and healthy eating diverted my attention from God and from the harsh reality that Zach was dying. In hindsight, I wish I had placed more emphasis on enjoying relationships and less on finding solutions. Thankfully, grace reminds me how Jesus will return wasted moments. He hushes my regret and guilt and promises me he will work all things out, even my worst moments. Any relationship damage caused by stress can be turned into beauty by God's great mercy. Without this knowing, I would be riddled with remorse over all I did wrong during our cancer journey.

Near the end of our season in Kelowna, I craved time and space to breathe, laugh and rest. Zach finished his treatments a week earlier than Doug and I longed to get home and be in my own bed and in familiar surroundings. I wanted to connect with friends and I desperately wanted to be with my children alone. Darcie agreed to come to Kelowna and stay with Doug while I went back to Kamloops with the boys. I felt so relieved. I would miss Doug and worry while being away, but I really needed a break and wanted the boys to have a rest without being inundated with treatments, diagnoses, doctors, and blood tests. I wanted to have moments that resembled life before cancer.

On Zach's last day of radiation, Darcie encouraged him to wear comical glasses with fake eyes painted on them. Everyone burst into laughter when he nonchalantly walked into the radiation waiting area. The radiologists tearfully said their goodbyes, handing him a Rocky Balboa greeting card that belted out the Rocky theme song. I was sure people in the waiting room were going to miss Zach's quirky, hilarious ways as well. He had an uncanny way of communicating and bringing laughter to people's lives as he engaged with them in conversations about whatever random facts came into his head. He loved to read about facts, whether in *Ripley's Believe It Or Not* or some fact app he found on his iPod. With his brain tumour, his filter system allowed him to say things that, normally, he would not dream of saying. He would blurt out things such as "Did you know that a guy from Sri Lanka can surf on his head for fifteen seconds at a time?" or "Did you know that the biggest baby ever born was seventeen pounds?" or even "Did you know that Hitler only had one testicle?" I remember one day when the room was somber and uncomfortably quiet, Zach started pressing all kinds of farts on this fart app he downloaded. *Are you kidding me?* I thought. I was completely embarrassed, but people found it refreshingly funny.

After returning home, Zach started going to school again on days when he felt good, and life started seeming semi-normal. Carter settled into grade five with an amazing teacher, Mrs. McCarthy, who became instrumental in supporting him during the hard times in the year ahead. Doug returned home, but he still could not eat. Tube feeding was still the only way he could get enough calories. He continued to take Dilaudid, an opioid pain medication, for his severe radiation burns. Dilaudid made him confused and perpetually tired, so he made the decision to come off of it. Doctors had emphasized the importance of tapering off medication slowly, but Doug, fed up with feeling "out of it," decided to come off Dilaudid completely, without weaning as doctors had suggested. After one day of coming off his meds, he began to experience unbearable withdrawal symptoms. Shivering and sweating all night long, he thought he was going to go mad. We would need to change our bed sheets throughout the night because of his night sweats. I was frustrated he had not listened to the doctor's advice. I was pulled and stretched in different directions. I wanted to create normalcy in my children's lives, but I also wanted to take care of Doug's needs. It all felt like ripping and tearing. On the one hand, I felt compelled to stay home with Doug, but on the other hand, I wanted to spend time with Zach and Carter away from the suffocating effects of cancer.

On a rainy day, the boys and I decided to put on our gumboots and search for mud piles to play in. Doug assured me he would be OK, so Zach, Carter and I made plans for an adventure. The hills in Kamloops are made up of clay hoodoos and when it rains they are slippery and fun to slide down. We drove out to Dallas, a suburb of Kamloops, and trekked to the top of the highest hoodoo. The rain pelted down, making perfect conditions for sliding through steep gulches. We would climb to the top and then fly down at top speed, laughing and treasuring our time together. Part way through, Doug called on my cell phone. He was not doing well. His anxiety had reached an all time high and he felt he needed to go to the hospital. All sorts of feelings warred within me. I was angry my time with Zach and Carter had been cut short and frustrated about Doug's unrelenting symptoms. With boots caked in mud on the outside, and hearts filled with muddy emotions on the inside, we made our way home. We went to the ER, and as I suspected, Doug was experiencing symptoms of anxiety. Weighed down with all of the complications of recovery, Doug decided it might be best if he stayed at his sister's place for a day so I could have a rest from caregiving. I was grateful he gave me this respite.

We all tried to find life's gifts in the ugliest of days, but often it felt like too much work. I found it hard to resist the urge to give in to the pain and admit we had lost the battle. We tried to live each day fully alive, but most days we were functioning at about twenty percent, optimistically. Zach still needed to do blood work, so dreaded visits to the hospital were necessary. The hospital smells of disinfectants mixed with turkey soup from the cafeteria made me want to throw up. Continually being poked with needles for blood work at the lab and for vitamin C and Elixir treatments at the naturopathic clinic traumatized Zach's veins. Nurses could not draw blood because his veins would hide, a common problem with cancer patients. We would put EMLA® on before we left home, an ointment to numb the site, but the psychological trauma from the needles caused a physical response. We found that drinking lots of water and doing jumping jacks before they drew blood made his veins a lot more cooperative.

Most days Doug slept, trying to recuperate from all his body had endured. He had lost over twenty pounds, and he resembled someone just out of a concentration camp. Whenever I looked at him, I felt debilitating fear: his eyes were drained of all hope. Fatigue, anxiety and depression clouded all his joy. Many times, he would try to participate in a family outing, only to start vomiting from over-exertion. Despite all Doug's challenges, he struggled to the front of our church one Sunday morning to sing Chris Tomlin's song *I Will Rise* to honour Zach's heroic battle against cancer. The music soothed and comforted us all. Doug reminded us that even though our hearts and bodies were failing us, Jesus anchored our souls. That day, were reminded that when Jesus did usher Zach into heaven, he would no longer experience sorrow and pain. The darkness would break to light, the shadows would disappear, and our son would overcome the grave, entering heaven and saying, after his long battle, "It is well." Stifling back tears, I was overwhelmed with love for Doug. He was declaring the opposite of what was happening in our lives. He was defying the pain in his body to honour our son. Up until that point, cancer had contaminated his every waking moment, but now he broke through the thick darkness with songs of praise.

...in his grace there is life;
weeping may be for a night,
but joy comes in the morning.

Psalm 30:5 (BBE)

CHAPTER 7

TIMES IN BETWEEN

"What did the world look like (its contours and colours) before the cyclones came, before storms kicked up ordinary time and twisted it, spindled it, into oblivion?"

—MaryAnn McKibben Dana

When you are in the eye of the storm, moments open up where there is peace and time to catch your breath before the cyclone hits again. While we were in that space between remission and recurrence, it was easy to forget that a storm was brewing. It felt like we could stay in that place forever and defy time. We had tastes of the storm, little wafts to remind us it lurked around the corner, but we could forget for a while that its fury would be arriving soon. Time slowed down enough for us to relish moments together.

Songwriter David Bailey, a twelve-year glioblastoma survivor, wrote a song called "If I Had Another," which reminded me how time is a beautiful essence when you do not know how much more of it you have. In this song, Bailey takes time and breaks it into moments of beauty. He says if he had another week, he would "fly down to Jamaica or catch a clipper off the coast of Maine," or maybe, instead, he would "take a train to California and find [his] way to the shade of the big trees and have a glass of wine [while writing] a song among the pines." If blessed with another hour he would make a pot of coffee and drink it slowly in his back yard. Even if he only had another minute he would put his arms around his baby and hold her like he had never done before. Bailey's song reminded me to live each day in the moment. This was easier said than done, but I craved for the wonder of each new day to be awakened in me, so cancer would not cloud everything. I needed to sift through my heart to see if there was anything left uncontaminated by pain, anything salvageable. I began to focus on the beauty around me—the design of a flower, the feeling of the breeze, the sound of a bird—and realized I still appreciated simple gifts in nature. Not all had been annihilated by pain and beauty still stirred my heart. On days when I found it hard to find peace, poetic descriptions of nature helped still my heart. Whenever I doubted that a more hopeful day would come, I would allow my imagination to take me to a place where tragedy did not exist. Imagination quelled the tides of grief.

One particular book, Anne Morrow Lindbergh's, *A Gift From the Sea*, activated all of my senses that had been buried under grief. Lindbergh, longing for solitude and time for contemplation, wrote her book while staying in a cottage on Captiva Island on Florida's Gulf Coast. Whenever I read the rich images she describes of the ocean, I felt my heart settle in spite of the painful circumstances surrounding me daily. I allowed Lindbergh's words to wash away the grit of cancer:

We awake to the soft sound of wind through the Casuarina trees and the gentle sleep-breathing rhythm of waves on the shore. We run barelegged to the beach, which lies smooth, flat, and glistening with fresh wet shells after the night's tides. The morning swim has the nature ot a blessing to me, a baptism, a rebirth to the beauty and wonder of the world. We run back tingling to hot coffee on our small back porch . . . with legs in the sun we laugh and plan our day."[1]

Lindbergh's language awakened something in me that had died. I made a point of carving out moments in my day to be outside so I could soak in God's goodness. Running made me feel more connected with God. Alone on the trails, I could sort through the chaos of my mind. I absorbed God's goodness in the warmth of the sun, listening to worship music playing on my iPod. My favourite worship album while running was Steven Curtis Chapman's *Beauty Will Rise*. Produced after the death of his daughter, the songs give voice to his family's grieving process. The lyrics were salve and hope to my heart. I felt healing from heaven with each step I took: beauty would rise and we would dance among the ruins. The songs were gentle waves, reminding me to take another breath and let the tears come. God's promises came like fresh rain and I sensed Jesus reaching for my face to wipe the tears away. Somehow, new life would shine and he would make a way for joy to come in the morning. I wanted to stay in this place of refreshing forever. Whenever I stopped running, my sadness would come back. When the music stopped, it seemed like God's love went with it. Moments, running in nature with God tucked in my heart, became my sanity.

One day, as I was heading to the car after a trail run, a monarch butterfly landed on my shirt. I gently took it off to examine carefully. God spoke gentle words to soothe and comfort, reminding me to slow down and notice life's details. A verse from the Song of Solomon flashed through my mind: "Look around you: winter is over; the winter rains are over, gone! Spring flowers are in blossom all over. The whole world's a choir—and singing! Spring warblers are filling the forest with song. Lilacs are exuberantly purple and perfumed, and the cherry trees fragrant with blossoms" (Song of Solomon 2:11-13 MSG). I breathed long, slow breaths and tried to let the hopeful words sink into my heart. Yet, somehow this promise still felt so far away, so unrealistic. I could not imagine this winter ending. I could not imagine spring.

Zach and I enjoyed hiking on the trails in Peterson Creek together, talking lazily about life. It felt great to slow down and sense the ambiance of spring with its new life. Zach could not walk very fast, so we would meander down the trail, oblivious of time, to our favourite spot which we called "Shrek's Swamp," enjoying the sun and the beautiful yellow Arnica flowers coming up. When you are not sure how much time is left for these moments, they become achingly special. I memorized Zach's step, body language, hair, and his special qualities, knowing that later I would have to rely on my memory to recall him—all the minute details that made him who he was. Sometimes he struggled with fatigue and had a difficult time catching his breath, but then he would get this look in his eye, and suddenly he would break out in a full run. I could not figure out what on earth he was doing. Why this sudden burst of liveliness? He was fed up with cancer and defiantly resisted its limitations by running in spite of weariness. I smiled to myself and thought, *Thataboy! You give it a run for its money.* Doug, Zach, and Carter also spent many hours in Peterson Creek shooting at targets of hilarious cartoon characters that Doug had sketched on paper. As long as Zach felt good, they would spend their afternoons shooting bows and arrows, laughing, and enjoying time in the woods together. The pinnacle of their shooting experiences came when Doug arranged for a friend to take the boys to the shooting range. Little did I know, their adventure involved shooting AK 47s. Not only were they hanging out in the woods shooting guns, they were also sneaking off for burgers and Blizzards behind my back. Had I known what they were up to at the time, I probably would have had a fit. I am sure as they were heading to A&W in their get-away car, they were all having a great laugh together.

We also cherished our times at Sun Peaks, skiing as a family. As soon as the inflammation from Zach's surgery had healed, we would go up every weekend together. Zach's fatigue made some days difficult, but occasionally he would have a surge of energy and would fly down the mountain like Evel Knievel. He surprised all of us one day when he announced he wanted to go down "Challenger." We had contemplated going down this double black diamond run with the boys but had never actually done it. We were a bit concerned because Zach tired so easily, but I sensed this was a bucket-list adventure, so we set out enthusiastically on our quest to overcome the most difficult run on the hill. One slow turn after another, with stops in between, he conquered it. This was one of many examples of Zach's tenacity throughout his cancer journey. Another time that stands out to me was when he made the decision to play basketball after his craniotomy. A few weeks after his surgery, his basketball team had a game in Logan Lake, which is about forty minutes away from Kamloops. I asked him if he would like to go and watch. He looked at me with his dancing, bright eyes and said, "No, I'd like to go and play." He battled fatigue throughout the game, but the sparkle in his eyes and his famous smile never faded for one moment. He had to sit on the bench more than the others, but he played all the way to the end, cheering on his team and playing his heart out. I cannot remember whether his team won the game or not. That was of no importance to me. All I remember was how proud of him I felt. Time and time again, God infused Zach with supernatural determination.

After all we had been through over the past few months, we hungered for a getaway. We decided to spend three days at Sun Peaks, enjoying hot tubs, cozy fires, eating out, and relishing the beautiful winter wonderland. Sun Peaks has Switzerland-style architecture, so when it is snowy, it has a fairy-tale feel. The first day, much to our dismay, we forgot Carter's snowboard and all of the food, so after an exchange where Doug and I blamed each other, and Carter rolled his eyes at the complete stupidity of his parents, we journeyed back down the mountain to find our stuff still on our front porch. We made it back in time for the last run of the day. We broke all our good eating habits and had chocolate, pizza, and ribs. Zach ate heartily, smiling from ear to ear over his good fortune. He was giddy over this new breakthrough in the food regime, and I think he wanted to stand up and shout, "Hallelujah!" at the top of his lungs.

As we pulled back the curtains the next morning, we were met with a foot of fresh powder. The snow fell lightly with bits of blue sky and sun peaking behind the clouds. The white sparkled diamond-like, a gentle reminder that God really does make everything new. Carter and Doug rushed to get ready and headed out, anticipating the best snow day of all time. I chuckled to myself and thought, *I wish Carter would move that fast to get ready for school.* I often wondered what would happen if our house ever caught on fire. He just does not hurry *ever.* Zach and I snuggled in bed for a few more hours and then made our way out. In spite of his enthusiasm, he tired quickly, so we returned to the condo and rented *The Princess Bride*, his favourite movie next to *Natcho Libre*. We had a fun-filled weekend, but I could tell it had taken its toll on Zach — he was more exhausted than usual.

When Darcie found out about Zach's prognosis, she made a referral to the Make-A-Wish Foundation to see if we would be eligible for going on a wish trip. The foundation quickly connected with us, setting a date to discuss Zach's dream wish. Two emotions battled within me: joy, about going somewhere special as a family, and sorrow, that we were going because of a life-threatening illness that would likely take my son's life. Without a second thought, Zach said Hawaii would be his wish. Make-A-Wish went overboard, giving both Zach and Carter spending money and extra little gifts, making them feel cared for and loved. Just before we left home, a huge box came to our house. It felt like Christmas as Zach and Carter went through the box containing all their special treats: *Pirates of the Caribbean* movies, photo albums, hockey figurines, Make-A-Wish backpacks, baseball caps, T-shirts, and much, much more. I loved how this organization included Carter in their generosity.

At the end of November 2009, we flew to Oahu for Zach's dream adventure. We stayed at the Waikiki Sunset hotel near the ocean. The warm Hawaiian weather, palm trees, and a stunningly beautiful ocean were such a welcome contrast to the below-freezing temperatures at home. The colours and smells were rich and refreshing. We arrived at our hotel energized with anticipation about what our week together would be like. Almost our entire extended family would be sharing in Zach's special week, and I think all of us had confusing feelings. Mixed with our excitement, we felt deep sadness. Likely this trip would be our last with Zach. In ways there was too much pressure to make it perfect. Zach also had ambivalent feelings. He felt his family's love and knew he was the guest of honour, cherished beyond measure. But I sensed he grieved for future trips that would be no more. Because of Zach's people-pleasing nature, I felt worried he was burdened to make this trip special for us. So many feelings bounced back and forth inside me.

On our first full day, we relaxed on the beach enjoying the waves, sun, sand, and connectedness of being together as one family. Every moment possible, I took snapshots, trying to capture and preserve the moments, while at the same time drinking it all in, our weary souls healing in this paradise. Hawaii stirred our spirits to life again. God seemed closer and miracles seemed possible here. Hope was resuscitated and sorrow put on hold. As I explored the world below the surface of the water, it was easy to forget that above the surface, cancer was our reality. Underwater, all was well. I relished the solitude where, for a while, I could soak in God's glory. His beauty surrounded me everywhere I looked; there was majestic, unadulterated beauty. The colours beckoned me to worship. I saw glimpses of heaven when I examined the details of fish swimming by, when I watched the slow, unhurried pace of a sea turtle, when I noticed the rich colours of the sea life in the reef, and when I swam free through the bright, clear blue water. I hesitated before lifting my head to break the surface because I knew I would have to face reality again.

My grief was quieted by simply playing together with my family, but sometimes sudden jolts would hit me out of nowhere: *This trip is because Zach is dying.* Nearly simultaneously, I felt peaceful and anxious. The ebb and flow of emotions were as constant as the waves hitting the shore. Captivated by our moments together, I was still aware cancer tainted my ability to stay in the moment. I realized sorrow this deep does not take a vacation; it just takes a backseat a certain times. I studied Zach's body language, interpreting his winces as pain came, sometimes aching pain and sometimes acute. I was aware I could not fully relax even though everyone else seemed relaxed around me. I probably drove Zach nuts barraging him with questions: "Zach, are you OK?" "Do you need more pain medication?" "How are your headaches?"

Zach and I had brainstormed two months before the trip about the excursions he wanted to do. He had chosen sailing, swimming with the dolphins, going on a submarine ride, and snorkeling at Hanauma Bay. When he had made these decisions, he had had enough energy, but now he felt exhausted and worn down. Chemotherapy, radiation, blood work, and doctors were not allowed on this holiday, yet the traumatizing effects of cancer came along with us. Fatigue made it difficult to do the very things he really wanted to do. Our trip to swim with dolphins turned into a scary ordeal. Just before Zach was to go into the pool, he buckled over with unbearable stomach pain. He and I walked around the property trying to breathe through the pain. He often developed a metallic taste in his mouth at random times that really upset him. Between this taste in his mouth and his debilitating pain, we did not think he would be able to participate in his wish. However, after twenty minutes the symptoms passed and he was able to join the dolphins. Later, his submarine excursion also came at a cost. Just as we climbed down the ladder into the submarine, Zach started having incapacitating headaches. Suddenly, my heart sank as I realized I had forgotten to give him his Decadron in the morning. Missing a Decadron dose can lead to headaches, double vision, slurred speech or even seizures. I could not believe I had forgotten. Each time Zach's symptoms reared their heads, a piece of my heart died.

Our most enjoyable days were the ones where we had no plans. Lazy days at the beach, without pressure to have wishes granted were the best. Some of our favourite times were evening dinners under beautiful sunsets. I loved watching Saige, Carter and Zach banter with each other at the table. The three of them would have contests to see who could stick a spoon on their nose for the longest time. Without fail, Zach won the contest. After seven gorgeous days, we boarded the plane to go home and, honestly, I was relieved. I had loved our time and valued it deeply, but I wanted to go back where we would be close to medical help if we needed it. Zach had been getting headaches throughout the trip, along with stomach pain and fatigue. His cancer was a time bomb, unpredictable and fierce, and we all needed the comforts of home.

My heart is full when I think of our moments in the eye of the storm, but nothing compares to the joy I felt when Zach and I were baptized on February 28, 2010. For whatever reason, I had never been water baptized, and finally it made sense: God had wanted me to wait so that during the last days of Zach's life, I would be able to share this intimate, life-changing moment with my son. The circumstances in our lives screamed that God had given up on us. The battle had taken its toll, and all of heaven held its breath waiting for our response. Together, he and I defied darkness. Like a vine that twisted its way into the fabric of our lives, cancer permeated every waking moment. But when Zach and I were baptized, it felt like the vine had been uprooted and severed somehow. In the days leading up to our baptisms, I fantasized about Zach coming out of the water healed. I felt disheartened when I still saw the lump on the side of his head when he emerged from the water. However, I sensed others were healed. I imagined all of heaven standing in a moment of silence to honour a valiant warrior.

As Zach shared his testimony in front of the church, words of his treasured verse from Isaiah touched every heart in the room, especially mine. *How could a thirteen-year-old boy boldly read this verse as his verse, specifically given to him by God?* He was dying of cancer—he only had three months to live—and he stood in front of an audience saying, "When I go through rivers of adversity, my Savior will rescue me." Courageously he took a stand, looked out at those gathered, and proclaimed God was bigger than cancer. God had things covered no matter how life looked. A megaphone of hope was telling the world cancer might have its way for a while, but it would not defeat him. I had seen what Zach had been through, his fear, discouragement and loneliness, yet he stood up and told people that God was with him. People's lives were being transformed by his faith and courage. Joy in the midst of suffering took on a whole new meaning, as seeds of love were spread out through Zach's testimony. All of the angels rejoiced because Zach had overcome death even though he was dying. Love had the final say.

Special moments between Zach and his Auntie Margie at Sun Peaks

Beautiful Sun Peaks, our favourite place to get away from it all

Zach enjoying a snack after a long day of skiing

Playing at Lac De Bois with Auntie and Saige

Uncle Shon and Zach rippin' on the Jet Ski during our family reunion at Okanagan Lake (two weeks after Zach's craniotomy)

Carter doing his favourite summer sport (other than longboarding) while listening to "Sweet Home Alabama" blaring out of the boat speakers

The smile Zach was known for

Enjoying a high-speed quad adventure with Grandpa Ralph

Zach shooting pellet guns in the backyard with Ryan

Shooting AK 47s at the shooting range

Darcie, Ryan, Kirsten, Saige, Carter, Zach, and myself
on Zach's Make-A-Wish trip

Carter, Zach, and Saige at Sunset Beach in Oahu

Sunset Beach, Oahu

*Grandma Rudy and Grandpa Ray during
our rained out luau*

Boogie boarding at Waikiki Beach

Carter and Zach snorkeling at Hanauma Bay, looking for sea turtles

*Saige, Carter, and Zach enjoying a sunset dinner
on the beach at Waikiki*

Grandma Laird with her boys

Zach clowning around at a restaurant in Oahu

He will come to us like the winter rains,
like the spring rains that water the earth.

—Hosea 6:3 (NIV)

CHAPTER 8

MY BOYS

"You'll miss the best things if you keep your eyes shut."

—Dr. Seuss

Life holds beauty even within the harshest conditions. As our family was being bombarded by life at every corner, I still found some happiness in day-to-day family life and in Zach and Carter's unique personalities. Carter is typically high-spirited and enjoys his role as the family comedian. Usually, his funny side makes it impossible to have a straight face around him. Even in the midst of trauma, his daily shenanigans, although sometimes inconvenient, were refreshing. On account of cancer, though, his silly moments had become less frequent. Doug and Zach's illnesses weighed heavily on his happy-go-lucky demeanor. Carter ached for how life had been before cancer. Zach no longer had as much energy to play with him and his special bond with Doug had been disrupted. Until now, he and Doug had loved wrestling, football, and playing goofy games together. In particular, they had enjoyed playing a ridiculous game they called "Mad Cow." In this game, all Doug had to do was yell, "Moo!" at the top of his lungs and the game would begin. He would chase Carter around the house pretending he had Mad Cow Disease. Now, These spontaneous fun moments together seemed to be things of the past. I could see the loneliness and fear in Carter's eyes as he watched Doug and Zach become sicker and sicker. He got angry easily and was often moody and withdrawn.

To help me understand what Carter was experiencing, a friend brought over a CD called *Unexpected Gifts*, which describes cancer's impact on different members of the family. During one of the scenarios on the CD, each member of the family was given an opportunity to speak about how cancer was affecting them. Chloe, the sibling of the child with cancer, shared what it was like to be the invisible one:

I asked Dad today if I could write something in the family journal. He said, "Of course you can—you are an important part of this family." Somehow it made me feel better to hear him say that because lots of days I kind of feel invisible. I can be talking to mom about something awesome and even though she's pretending to listen, she just isn't paying attention. Sometimes I even say something weird just to test her, but mostly she doesn't notice. I wonder if it would be selfish to write down how much that bugs me. It is so hard having my brother sick like this. I miss being able to play with him and not feel like I have to let him win. I can't even fight with him anymore without someone telling me to be careful that I don't upset my brother. Sometimes I think, well, what if I get upset, would you even notice? But then I feel guilty. It is very confusing."

Like Chloe, Carter often felt invisible. People constantly scurried around getting Doug and Zach pain relievers, cleaning up vomit, and phoning doctors. Did anyone care about Carter? When life starts to weigh him down, Carter often blurts out things before he has time to sort his thoughts out in his head. On one particular day, my bad mood collided with his, and it was toxic. Carter informed me that his life "sucked" and started packing his bags to move out. Under normal conditions, I would have cuddled him, tuned into him, and reassured him, but on this day, I got the worst mother of the year award. I looked at him and said, "I think that is a good idea. How about I go warm up the car?" Gritty exchanges like this became normal when trauma was what we woke up to every day.

Carter and I laugh about this shared moment of ugliness now, but at the time, neither one of us found anything humourous about the situation. Although emotional pain and family upheaval pushed against Carter daily, he continued to participate in soccer, basketball, volleyball, and wrestling. When I could go and just watch him be Carter, doing what he loved, there were small amounts of joy and normalcy. Like Carter, I too longed for how life used to be. The way Carter and I relate to each other flourishes when we can share adventures together. Needless to say, cancer often sabotaged special times that made our hearts come alive. We did manage to get out skiing, hiking, tobogganing, and playing, but a crisis of some sort usually ended the fun abruptly. Carter became apprehensive about doing family outings because inevitably our time would end in disappointment when either Doug or Zach would have pain we could not control.

To satisfy our yearning for fun, Carter and I made plans to go on a biking trip to Silver Star in Vernon. The two of us struggle with planning, generally, so, as usual, we left on our quest hopelessly unprepared. We did not think to layer up with warm clothing — who thinks of that in the summer?—and about twenty minutes into our long-awaited road trip, it started pour. We thought about turning around to get warmer things, but being the optimists we are, we convinced ourselves the rain would turn into sunshine. We pulled into the parking lot to find out the chairlift had broken down when the storm had blew a tree over the power lines. Rationally, I thought we should really get in the van and drive home, but the neglected fun part of me thought, *No way! We are not turning around.*

This day is not going to end how our adventures typically do. We are going biking, no matter what! I told Carter to gear up because nothing would get in the way of our plans. To our delight, the chair re-opened. We could barely contain our joy.

So, off the two of us went, happy and unprepared in our cotton shirts and shorts. Halfway up the chairlift, we started shivering uncontrollably as the rain came down in sheets and the wind blew without mercy. We flew down our first run, nearly hypothermic and barely able to hang on to our handlebars or brakes. As soon as we got to the bottom, we went into the village frantically searching for warm clothes. Too cold to price check or try on clothes, we haphazardly grabbed whatever off the shelf. I mistakenly got Carter an XL fleece that he will be able to wear into adulthood. The storeowner mercifully gave us some large garbage bags to put over our clothes as raingear. Before venturing out again, we decided to go back to the minivan, fuel up on pepperoni and popcorn, and watch *Invictus* on our little video machine. We cranked up the heat so our gloves and clothing would dry out, and an hour later, we were back on the trails, hooting and hollering as we hit the tabletops and banked corners. Before long, we had dirt in our teeth and up our noses. By the end of the day, every nook and cranny of our bodies was bogged down with mud. It felt wholesome to step into another world for a while and spend uninterrupted time with Carter.

Carter also seemed happier when he could spend time with his cousin Saige. In the same way Margie brought hope to my heart, Saige brought new life to Carter. She stepped into spots that normally Zach would have filled, longboarding, playing Legos, roughhousing and doing activities she knew Carter loved. One night, after dinner, Saige bet Carter two dollars that he would not dress up as a girl and go play basketball on the street. Sporting high heels and a dress, and wearing makeup, he went out to shoot hoops in the front yard for all to see. Our family coped with many hard times using humour, and once again, Saige's dare brought much-needed comic relief for our family. While they played and bantered most of the time, on occasion, Saige would step into a mothering role with Carter, sensing he needed to be nurtured. She intuitively knew how my emotional absence was affecting him and she tried to fill in the gap. In her kindness, she attempted to organize Carter, going to his classes with him, helping him with his homework, and attempting to improve his study habits. But he tended to go against the grain, and could, at times, frustrate Saige. They would get in some grandiose fights due to Carter's lack of compliance, but regardless of their squabbles, Saige's presence really helped Carter navigate through some very dark times.

Like Carter, Zach also revelled in one-on-one time with family members. Ryan, Kirsten and Darcie would make a special effort to spoil Zach when they came for visits. Zach knew he would be able to talk them into all sorts of fun outings. He persuaded Ryan and Kirsten into taking him to Montanas for ribs, and he convinced Darcie to take our Nissan Z to Merritt with the top down, blasting Bob Marley the whole way. They topped off their adventure with burgers and Dairy Queen Blizzards, of course. Whenever Zach went on outings with people, he convinced them he had never had a Blizzard in his life, and, of course, his wish was their command. A newspaper photographer, next door to our house, organized a ride for Zach in a Lamborghini, thinking that would be every kid's dream. I became increasingly concerned when they were not home on time. Finally they pulled into the driveway and Zach emerged, smiling ear to ear, with a large Blizzard in his hand. His Lamborghini experience paled in comparison to the joy of his Blizzard.

Given what both of my children were going through, I marvelled at their abilities to squeeze happiness out of life's simple pleasures. Nothing gave Zach greater joy than food. Zach's appetite amused a lot of his friends. One of his buddies, Ty Fuoco, had him over to hang out, and later his mom Diane sent me a card that made me smile. She wrote: "When Zach came over the other day, the boys went bike riding, and when they got back, Zach found his way to the kitchen and I gave him a drink. I was making some hotdogs for dinner, and he said, 'Boy, those look good,' so I offered him one. He took it and went to watch TV with Ty. Then he wandered back into the kitchen—I could see it in his eyes—'Zach, do you want another one?' Three hotdogs later, he asked me what time it was. I told him it was just after five o'clock and he said, 'Oh man, I gotta go! I don't want to be late for dinner.'"

Along with his ferocious appetite, Zach had a hunger for adventure. He enjoyed camping, exploring, travelling, and road trips. We went to the Bike Ranch in Kamloops shortly after his craniotomy. He flew down the hill faster than I had ever seen him ride before. I nearly had a fit as he launched himself off teeter-totters and tabletops. I tried to keep up with him, all the while praying fervently, "Jesus, slow him down!" Jesus did not slow him down, but he did keep him from crashing and causing irreparable harm.

Another favourite activity for Zach was our annual family reunion on Okanagan Lake at his Uncle Shon's place. Before a visit, Shon would send the boys a note to build excitement for the occasion, such as this one:

Heya, boys! Looking forward to a visit. Maybe we can hit the local bar for a few drinks, grab some R-rated horror movies and then head downtown and get a couple of full-length back tattoos. Then we can hit six or seven fast food joints, buy every combo they have, blend them into smoothies and drink them (with a very small amount of wheatgrass to make your mom happy). You should practice up on your UFC moves, too, because I am brushing off some new holds to test out on you boys. Most of them involve some degree of chokes and joint locks so eat your shark cartilage and Flintstone chewables.

Plenty of hugs, your semi-favourite semi-uncle.

P.S. If you're ever up all night and can't sleep, CALL ME! I mean it! We can laugh and talk about all the ways we can scare the wits out of your mom.

Shon's humour felt like fresh rain. Both of the boys thought Shon acted like comedian Chris Farley. Being with him allowed them to forget about all their worries as he entertained them with funny, albeit often inappropriate, humour. On one of our visits, he convinced Zach and Carter to eat a box of Vivapuffs, telling them the real name was Vitapuffs. He promised them I would not mind because *vita* meant that the marshmallow, jam-filled cookies were full of nutritious vitamins. Along with practical jokes, Shon thrilled Zach and Carter with adventurous activities. At Okanagan Lake, he would take them out on jet skis, open up the throttle, and give them the ride of their lives. He satiated their hunger for fun. Even when Shon was not with Zach and Carter, he showed them he cared by having gifts delivered to our home. Knowing how much Zach loved Legos, Shon had his dream project delivered by Purolator: the Star Wars Death Star and the Millennium Falcon. Shortly after the Star Wars surprise, he delivered a longboard for Carter. Shon tuned in to their hearts and quieted the effects of cancer with his uncanny way of connecting with them.

Like Shon, Zach understood how to combine humour with sensitivity. He had deep wells of compassion for others and for the world around him. When our family worked at the Anglican Church's Out of the Cold program, providing shelter to the homeless in the winter, Zach would laugh, strike up conversations with street people, and be very aware of their needs. They would tell Zach their life stories, drawn to him because he cared beyond his years. Even as a young child, Zach had been able to discern the feelings of others. During the final days of Jay's illness, I had struggled to get him into the bathroom, and little, sensitive Zach had come to the rescue, reassuring and comforting Jay with his little teddy bear. Sometimes his sensitivity had made it difficult for him to cope. Once, in his kindergarten year, I picked him up after school and found him deeply disturbed. I thought maybe he had been bullied, but his sadness came from his fear that kids were hurting the branches of a willow tree when they were swinging on its limbs. The thought of squishing bugs or hurting any living creature grieved his heart. Jay was held back in grade one for being too sensitive, and I had struggled with it all of my life. Zach had inherited our gift.

Added to Zach's sensitivity was his first-born confidence and attention to detail. He had a firm handshake, looked people in the eye, and connected to them by focusing on their interests instead of his own. Of course, he did not always exhibit these mature qualities. Right up until a few days before he died, we could hear him singing in the shower with abandon and doing armpit farts. He had a beautiful mixture of silliness and wisdom. Like many first-borns, Zach liked to be exacting and precise. His drawings, for example, were intricate and meticulous. He had a keen eye for colours and textures. He also had a strong desire to please others. Carter, by comparison, liked to draw outside the lines, driving Zach nuts. The day Doug and I married, Carter became obsessed with going to play in the sand. Because he did not get his way, he rebelliously turned his head away from the camera whenever we were trying to get family pictures. Zach stood beside him, forcing his head toward the camera. It was comical to watch a six-year-old trying to rein in a four-year-old.

Because Zach was so particular, he could get agitated when things did not go the way he planned. For example, he struggled with teamwork. He preferred to do projects alone, where he could do things in his own systematic way. If he was working on a Lego project or on a drawing design and someone interfered with his flow, he would become deeply frustrated. Even though Zach loved people, he was an introvert. He valued his alone time. Usually the fights between he and Carter were due to Carter's extroversion. Carter *loved* spending time with Zach, and the most common thing we would hear coming from Zach's room was "Carter-man, could you please give me some time to myself?" When Zach had been three years old, I built him a sanctuary in the closet. His brother lived to get into his business, so I devised a plan to help him escape whenever he needed to. We put him and all his Legos in the closet, so he could enjoy part of the day in his quiet haven. He frequently asked, "Mom, can you put me in the closet?"

Zach's excellent imagination allowed him to experience his world in a more three-dimensional way than most. I would often find his imaginary worlds created in my plants. He would use dental floss to create zip lines and use plastic army guys to create military sieges. At three years old, he disappeared while was doing some work around the house. Alarmed by the quietness, I went searching for him, but could not find him anywhere. After what felt like forever, there was a knock on my door. One of the neighbors had found him downtown on his tricycle. As usual, his inquisitive mind had enticed him to go explore his world. When he was about four years old, he created an imaginary friend named John Jack who would take him on all sorts of expeditions to far-away places. His curious, scientific mind had needed to touch, collect, and examine. When I cleaned his room, I would find weird little experiments and odd collections of unusual things stored in little containers. Science captivated him. He loved to read about the human body. At six years old, he looked up from watching television and asked me what an epiglottis was for.

When I would get upset with Zach, it was usually because of his disorganization. He struggled when it came to planning. His imagination would get the better of him, and he would forget he actually lived in this world where he was required to get tasks done. He enjoyed daydreaming so much, he found it hard to focus on the moment. My favourite children's book is *Harold and the Purple Crayon* by Crockett Johnson. With only a purple crayon, Harold creates his reality by drawing pictures of what he wants to happen next in life. Like Harold, Zach learned how far his imagination could take him, and he created wonderful make-believe worlds in his mind that others could not see or understand. To many, he just seemed unfocused. At school, he would create pen rockets instead of listening to the teacher, probably imagining what it would be like to be an astronaut. He would cram papers into his desk until they compacted like a concrete slab. Rote math and worksheets did not fit in with his "out of the box" way of looking at the world, so he shoved school assignments aside because he was fantasizing of bigger dreams. He was not being deliberately defiant; he just had other, deeper thoughts that needed his attention. I remember his learning assistance teacher saying he was bright enough to be a doctor, but he would need to have a very good secretary. People with his level of imagination and intelligence see the world differently than most.

Cancer could not destroy the parts of my children's personalities that had been unique to them since they were born. Because Zach and Carter were able to get out of their heads and appreciate life's simple joys as they had done before cancer, I could do it more easily, too. Cancer had forced me to live in my head, but Zach and Carter pulled me back into my heart with their special ways of filtering life. Just when life seemed unbearable, they would suggest a fun idea that transcended the sadness in our hearts. One of Zach and Carter's favourite family activities during cancer treatments was playing "Guitar Hero" and "Rock Band" with their Nintendo Wii. Even when Zach was tired, he still had the energy to play, so we could all participate. The four of us would choose our instruments, either the bass guitar, lead guitar, drums or vocals. Using the Wii controllers, modelled after musical instruments, we would simulate popular rock music songs. We sounded horrible, but we loved the lightheartedness of the game. Zach and Carter's enthusiasm reminded me that our family life had not been reduced to facts, prognoses and to-do lists. Their personalities buoyed the heavy cancer atmosphere and wove into my pain like balm.

My boys having a tussle

Carter adventuring in the mountains

And now my life drains out, as suffering seizes and grips me hard.
Night gnaws at my bones; the pain never lets up.

—Job 30:16 (MSG)

CHAPTER 9

THE ABSENCE OF LIGHT

"The grief of it all, the despair and anger and guilt and powerlessness swirl together to cast a spell of numbness on your being. Your mind is dazed. Your capacity to notice, to connect, to feel — to feel alive, to feel others, to feel anything — slows like molasses in winter as the hurt dissolves the colour of a rose, and the world becomes essentially joyless."

— C. Baxter Kruger, *The Shack Revisited*

After a very short time of remission, Zach came into the kitchen one morning to show me a small, soft lump on his temple. I tried to calm my racing thoughts by assuring myself it was an infection developing at the radiation site. I took him down to the Urgent Care Walk-In Clinic to see if the doctor could drain it. I gave the physician Zach's history, and I could tell by the look on his face that he knew it was not an infection. I had talked myself into believing that the solution was simple:

we would go into the clinic, have it drained, and resume our normal activities. An MRI was ordered for December 30th, 2009. I felt sick. *Here we go again,* I thought. *Another tidal wave.* The grim reality was that all those days in Kelowna having radiation and chemotherapy amounted to a waste of our time.

A pastor in town, Nolan Clark, writes, "Everyone has a giant to kill. It just takes some faith, some fierce, fierce faith. Risk it all and the giant will fall." We had risked it all—everything— and our giant stood as tall and as intimidating as ever. I had been fasting and praying, weeping to God to align Zach's cells with heaven. But we heard nothing from heaven, absolutely nothing. A story in Brennan Manning's book, *Patched Together,* expressed the pain I felt about God's silence. The main character in the story, Willie Juan, experiences a blow of rejection and anguish that leaves his emotions reeling. Willie Juan had been subject to rejection and bullying throughout his young life because of his crooked leg and scars. Then, one day he meets Jesus and Jesus promises he will take care of him and be his friend. He gives Willie a bottle of amorine, the medicine of love. He promises him this medicine has healing power. Excited about his new friend Jesus and the bottle of amorine, Willie Juan goes home to put drops of amorine on his scarred body, but when he does, nothing happens. Even worse than seeing his scars unhealed is the sudden pain of betrayal he feels. He screams to Jesus, "I should never have trusted you…You're a faker, a phony! You lied to me?"[1] Like Willie Juan, I trusted God's medicine of love would heal Zach, yet Zach kept getting worse. Being able to see the tumour on the outside of Zach's head made me hate it even more than before. Every time I looked at Zach and saw the growing lump, I realized God was not answering my prayers, and like Willie Juan, I felt tricked and deceived. It was like the enemy was mocking me and taunting me, "Where is your God now? Why isn't he helping you? Your child is going to die, and God is doing nothing about it." All I saw were splatters of disappointment, and if I had been brave enough, I might have said out loud, "God, I hate you!" But I was not.

Doubt germinated at a frightening speed. My life was the perfect habitat for doubt seeds to thrive. Each day brought new questions and uncertainties. Perhaps what I had believed all along was not worth believing, especially if these were the results. I wanted to cordon off my doubt because I hated the fact I even doubted, but I could not help it. My sorrow contaminated how I saw God. A devotional by Ann Voskamp helped me understand how it was okay to doubt. Voskamp declares:

[I] won't shield God from [my] anguish by claiming He's not involved in the ache of this

world...the God who governs all can be shouted at when I bruise, and I can cry and I can howl and He embraces the David-hearts who pound hard on His heart with their grief and I can moan deep that He did this . . . I feel Him hold me — a flailing child tired in Father's arms."[2]

Voskamp's words were fresh and reassuring: I had permission to be mad at God because in his kindness, he heard my shouts as prayers. When I opened my bruised heart to him, he met my anger, disappointment and doubt with love. My guttural cries did not turn him away from me; they caused him to run to me in my distress and hold me until the night would break through to day. My raw, honest emotions released the angels to come and minister to me.

Sometimes we think God is like us. We transfer our fickleness onto him. When others yell at us, we pull away. When people do not measure up to our expectations, we often become angry and disappointed. But God is not fickle. He never changes. He always loves and there is nothing we can do to stop him from loving us. Our messiness only makes him more compelled to step in and rescue us when we are in trouble. Hiding under tidy prayers during our times of weeping undermines the relationship we have with God. When I complain to God that his promises in the Bible do not match up with my painful experiences, he not only invites my questions, but also encourages them. He does not want us to hold anything back from him. Relationships that fear confrontations are stunted. Marriages end in divorce when couples cannot be real with one another. The same is true with God. When we are not real with him, our relationship cannot grow and prosper. My relationship with God felt solid enough that I could be angry with him, yet not fear I was destroying our relationship. Angry prayers turned into fits of crying and my tears became my prayers.

As heaviness and doubt imprisoned me, I longed to get away. I looked up from my computer at a boat painting Carter did in grade one, and I wanted to jump on it and sail away. Jesus whispered, "Where would you go, Dana?" I pondered . . . I would sail away to an island with a cottage that had flowers coming out of the window boxes—an island away from all the heaviness. In my imagination, I pictured myself parking my boat and meandering up the path to the porch, where Jesus sat in a rocking chair, eyes gentle and inviting. His eyes met mine, and he asked, "What do you want?" "I want you to read me a story Jesus." He gently smiled, "What story would you like me to read to you, child?" I thought for a moment, and suddenly the story *Guess How Much I Love You*, by Sam McBratney came to mind. I had not read this story since Zach and Carter were little, and the fact Jesus brought it to mind lightened my heavy heart. Throughout the story, the dad rabbit outdoes the baby rabbit in acts of love.

When I had tucked Zach and Carter in at night and read them this story all those years ago, I had felt close and connected with them, as if time stood still and preserved moments of innocent, pure love between a mom and her boys. We had snuggled, tickled, and nestled into warm blankets, safe, secure, and attached to each other. Now, Jesus spoke life-giving words as he read me this story. He loved me intimately. He held me close to his heart. He was not even a breath away.

As December 30th approached, my fear increased. Zach had been getting increasingly more headaches and nausea. I knew it was not good. I hated the thought of going to the hospital again. As our familt made our way to the waiting area for Zach's MRI on that dreaded day, we picked a number and sat down, alone with our thoughts taking us to terrible places. Before going to the hospital, we had given Zach Ativan to help him cope with claustrophobia in the MRI machine. I wished I could give him an anesthetic to wipe out this memory altogether. When he had been four years old, he had fallen out of a tree fort and we had rushed to the hospital for stitches. After the ordeal, the nurses had given him some sort of concoction to help him forget about the trauma. I wished the nurses could induce amnesia now—for all of us. After the MRI, we were told to wait for someone to meet with us to discuss the results. We had to wait for what felt like forever because doctors needed to call in radiologists, oncologists, and surgeons. The waiting was the worst. The kids were playing games on their iPhones, and I sat in a dazed stupor, part of me wanting to prolong hearing the news and the other part of me just wanting to get it over with.

After about four hours of waiting, the same doctor who had been at Urgent Care the day I had taken Zach in to see if the lump was an infection started walking toward us. "Mrs. Goodman and Mr. Goodman?" Just the way he said it made me want to cry. We both stood up, and I instinctively told Doug to stay with the boys. I wanted to talk with the doctor alone to buffer anything he might say that would wound my already vulnerable and broken family. I was pulled into the "bad news" room, yet again. The doctor looked like he was going to cry, which I appreciated. At least I knew he was meeting me on a human level, not on a "case" level. "It is not good," he said. "There is a lot of tumour growth, and the lump on the outside is also tumour." His words pounded hard and hurt so much. *No, God, not my little boy! Not Zach! Not after all he has been through.* The cruel reality hit me like a tsunami. The doctor asked if I wanted him to tell Zach the news. "No, thank you." I walked to the door, struggling with each step. I conjured up resilience and commanded myself to pull it together. Our sons had heard too much bad news already, and I made a decision that day to walk out of the hospital and act like all was well. I refused to let my family see despair on my face. The honesty I felt compelled to live by during the first diagnosis left me. I gathered everyone, told them the doctors might be removing the lump, and then drove home, no questions asked. Zach always asked questions, but he did not ask a thing that night. I could not wait until Zach and Carter went to bed so I could cry.

Holding it in was choking me, and the violent shock of the news needed to be released from my body. I went downstairs to my office and howled to God. Release! Release! Release! No matter how much pain I cried out, I could not free the torment from my body. It was stuck in me. *God, get it out of me! I can't live like this. It is too much, God. Do something!!* I felt panicked and utterly forsaken. My children slept and for now they were safe, each in their own rooms, protected under duvet covers, but what would happen next? The thoughts flooded torrential: *What if Zach suffers horribly? How do I still his terror? How do I explain all of this to him? How will I live seeing his drawings, his Lego creations, his clothes, his shoes, his bed and his little tidbit creations all over the house when he is no longer here?* It dawned on me that soon I would not hear his overly energetic "Hello!" in the morning followed by the sound of rummaging, as he would look for the perfect Lego piece. I would not hear him bounding into the house after school, shouting, "Hey, Mom! How was your day?" All the losses pounded on me like an avalanche. *How will I ever be able to handle seeing Carter without him?* Doug came downstairs to hold me, his pain mixing with mine, and I felt his strength. Even though he was so weak, I knew he would never leave me, and we would share this journey together in all its awful grittiness. Bruised and broken, we were together. I sensed Jesus wiping our tears. He looked into our aching hearts and wept along with us.

Shortly after the MRI, Dr. Cochrane called. He had some scans he wanted to show us via email. I stayed on the phone while he sent me the images. He showed us the parts that were tumour and the parts that were tissue damage from radiation. He felt that it was worthwhile to go in and de-bulk the mass, which would mean a second craniotomy, another three-hour brain surgery. On the day Dr. Cochrane told us about the second surgery, I wrote in my journal, "No matter what life throws at us, our family will stand by this verse: 'O God, you are [our] God; [we] earnestly search for you. [Our] soul thirsts for you; [our] whole body longs for you in this parched and weary land where there is no water. [We] have seen you in your sanctuary and gazed upon your power and glory. Your unfailing love is better to [us] than life itself; how [we] praise you. [We] will honour you as long as [we] live, lifting up our hands to you in prayer'" (Psalm 63:1–4). Declaring those verses, even when my emotions did not line up with that promise, rattled the darkness. Friends started a prayer chain that would take place for twelve hours during Zach's surgery. Each person took a thirty-minute prayer slot so Zach would be covered in continual prayer. Friends cushioned our pain.

Doug, Zach, and I arrived in Vancouver on January 2nd, 2010. Zach's appetite could not be satiated due to the Decadron he was taking, so he ate like a shark at feeding time. Shortly after getting his IV and doing blood work, we received his food order: Subway and sushi. Strangely, Zach's mood was light, and he did not seem fearful of the surgery. It felt like God supernaturally sheltered him from all fear. The terror thrashed wildly in me, but he seemed peaceful. I thought of Carter at home alone, having to go to school while we were all here, and I realized I had made a mistake by not bringing him. I had thought it best at the time, but he was away from us, wondering, fearing, and dreading the next chapter in our story.

Two neurosurgeons came in to speak with Zach and explain their purposes for the surgery along with some of the risks. I appreciated how they looked at Zach when they were explaining the operation. So many other doctors had talked about him as though he were not in the room. These surgeons understood the importance of valuing Zach's wisdom and ability to understand hard realities. As I listened to the risks, every word created another scar on my heart: hemorrhaging, seizures, cognitive deficits, brain swelling, leakage of cerebrospinal fluid, paralysis, speech difficulties, and coma. *Is this assault on his brain worth it for a few more months?* I wondered. I wanted to vomit. Surely God was not seeing and hearing what I was seeing and hearing. All these dark detours, all this ugliness, stealing my son's childhood and his life. I hated this place. The dark unknown, day after day and week after week. Doug was silent, trying to contain his pain. Zach listened, and it seemed like the risks the doctors were spouting off were water off a duck's back to him and, once again, I did not understand. I wanted to soothe the pain and promise him I would not let them hurt him. I wanted to shake him awake, "Zach! Zach! This is a nightmare. You are safe; you were just having a bad dream." But this room, these surgeons, and these risks were all real. Meanwhile, Zach simply loved his Subway sandwich. He had learned to be fully present in each day, hour, and moment, and in this moment, his sandwich rocked.

After the doctors left, I felt uncontrollable sorrow welling up in me. I cried out to Jesus, *I'm not going to make it!* I sensed him walking through the hospital walls and my heart walls to rescue me. An image came to me: Jesus carrying me in his arms, his tears pouring down on me. He wept loudly as he took my pain onto himself. He whispered, "Every incision, every chemo treatment, every night filled with anguish, every heartbreaking test result—all of it, Dana—I felt it in my own body. I am going to avenge this. I have collected every tear in a bottle, and I am going to make this right. This fight is mine. At every crossroad of your life and your family's lives, my spirit will be there to direct you. I will give you the strength to pass the breaking point and not break." As he looked at me, his weariness reflected my pain. He had absorbed my heartache. The lyrics of Mark Schultz's song, "He's My Son," came to mind and I personalized them: *Jesus, can you hear me? [Zach] needs your help. I am not sure if I am getting through, but he is not just anyone; he is MY son.* Jesus whispered back to me, "He is my son, too. What hurts his heart hurts mine even more. What Zach is going through, what you all are going through, saddens me more than you know. I am with you. The peace you see in Zach is because I am sheltering him. He is safe in my arms. I will hold him during the surgery tomorrow and I will keep him safe. Do not be afraid."

Even though I sensed the presence of Jesus then, I could not stop the hammering of dark thoughts. Doug left to go spend the night at his brother's home. I felt alone and crushed in my spirit. Nights in the hospital were my most lonely times. The stillness of that night exaggerated sounds of pain coming from Zach as he slept. My body slowed down but my mind picked up speed, dark thoughts tumbling around with no boundaries. Fear stalked me at night. Even at home my nights were lonely and scary. I no longer slept in our bed. Each night I would curl up beside Zach's bed on a futon, wanting to be nearby in case he seized or was in pain or was afraid. When he would moan or get restless in his sleep, I knew he needed more pain meds. Attuned to every little sound he made, I was able to interpret his different types of pain. I struggled every night, but this night, the night before his surgery, was worse than any I had experienced so far. To calm my nerves, I crawled into my pink Valentine pajamas Doug had bought me, thankful to have something cozy in this place of broken dreams. Restless and agitated, I knew sleep would not come. Zach seemed peaceful, so I went down to the computer cubicle to check my blog.

Before leaving Kamloops, I had created a blog on a site called CaringBridge so our community could stay updated on what was happening in our lives. People could go on and post as guests and send us prayers and words of encouragement. CaringBridge worked brilliantly as a way to communicate and stay connected with the outside world. I was overcome with thankfulness on that night in particular when I saw people's kind words. Love and loyalty emerged like a beam of light. In the middle of hell, our community encircled us. Jesus revealed his heart to us through their hearts. I let the words comfort my ache. Here are a few poignant entries:

Dana, I wanted to let you know I am praying for your family. It is staggering to me when I hear of what burdens others are asked to carry and I am amazed always at how the family of God gathers around those who are in battle. Know that God cares deeply and has called many servants to come alongside your family to stand in the throne room and ask for a miracle. So, I am one of those in the family who is going to stand with you. I pray that the God of all comfort will draw you close and meet you at every moment with the grace, strength and endurance that you need every moment of every day. And I pray that Zach would be filled with all knowledge and understanding of how much he is loved.

Love, Tracey Dahl

I am praying for doctors to be guided with great wisdom and for God to give you peace and strength to stand alongside with hope in your heart. "For the joy of the Lord is [your] strength" (Nehemiah 8:10). I pray that as quickly as a scary thought would enter your mind, you would see God holding you all in his hand where peace and joy replace any anxiety or fear. Zach, you are a hero and the whole world is cheering you on and praying that soon you will be wolfing down giant burgers . . . Hang in there buddy — I can't wait to see that beautiful smile of yours.

John and Laurie Simonin

Friends' words felt like an oasis in a very dry desert. Gifts and words of encouragement fell like manna from heaven. Zach and Carter's classes at school had made a quilt of comfort for Zach called "Leaves of Love." Each child had designed their own leaf and then individual leaves had been sewn together to create a quilt. We felt protected by a human shield of friendship. I sensed the ladder Jacob saw in his dream in Genesis, with angels ascending and descending from heaven, delivering prayers and sending out God's answers to those prayers. I went back to bed, more at peace knowing angels were going up and down heaven's ladder, interceding on our behalf.

The next morning, we took Zach down to surgery, and he walked down the hallway like he owned the place. He was dominating darkness, telling it a thing or two with his confident body language. Nothing could take my courageous hero down. His comment as he walked down the hallway was, "Boy, I'm hungry; I can't wait to have a hamburger." His second comment was, "How exactly do they get that catheter in?" *Are you kidding me? Is this really what he is thinking about?* I marvelled. Romans 8:38 promises that "the one who died for us — who was raised to life for us! — is in the presence of God at this very moment sticking up for us. Do you think anyone is going to be able to drive a wedge between us and Christ's love for us? There is no way!" The enemy had not been able to drive a wedge between Zach and Jesus. Zach's peace overshadowed fear because he sensed God interceding on his behalf. There was no way a twelve-year-old should be radiating peace, boldly walking down the corridors for his second craniotomy. Jesus had him in his arms of love, and he was not letting go. I had shaky faith at best, but Zach was being protected and the thickest darkness could not bring him down. We waited in the hallway until the anesthetist brought us in. We put on masks and gowns and went in with Zach. We held his hand while the doctor injected the anesthetic. He slipped into unconsciousness. Dr. Cochrane made eye contact with me, behind his magnetized surgical glasses, and the surgical team took Zach away.

Doug and I went over to Starbucks and sat in silence . . . waiting . . . not knowing . . . staring numbly at nothing. Zach had gone in at 9 a.m., and at 2 p.m. we were finally able to go into the ICU to see him. He was coming off the sedatives, so he had no filter system whatsoever. He blurted out all sorts of quirky parenting things I had done. He looked at me and said, "Hey, Mom. Remember the time you got so mad at me and Carter-man you threw a pen at us and hit us in the head?" I replied, "As a matter of fact, I do, and let's not broadcast it to the world." Zach and Carter had always started fighting as soon as I was on the phone. On that occasion, I had given them the "stink eye", and they were not getting it, so I had hurled a pen at them, not thinking I would actually nail them with it. Now, I was laughing at my conscientious, sensitive boy being able to blurt out whatever was on his mind. It reminded me of the movie *Liar, Liar* when Jim Carrey could not keep his inside thoughts from recklessly spilling out of his mouth. Zach said many other hilarious (albeit, embarrassing) things that split my hidden faults wide open. In spite of feeling exposed though, I invited the comic relief.

The next day, nurses moved Zach from ICU into a private, comfortable room we could make homey and personalize so it felt less sterile and medical. Zach's eyes were completely swollen shut, and his spirits were really low. He was tired of the fight. His whole head was wrapped in gauze, and he kept trying to rip it off. It was making him itchy, sweaty and generally agitated and restless. Thankfully, the swelling soon went down enough for him to watch *Jurassic Park*, a nice distraction. While he was watching his movie, the oncologist called us in for a meeting. He seemed emotionally disconnected. As the meeting progressed, it took everything in me to restrain myself from jumping over the table and shaking him. Angry thoughts pulsed in my mind. *Do you know this is my son? He likes biking, hanging out with his friends and skiing. Up until a few months ago, his biggest worry was finding a missing school assignment, and now he has to endure this! He is not a case! Why is it when you go into his room to visit, you do not know what to say to him? Why is it your awkwardness is so painfully obvious? After your 'protocol' we go home and live out this nightmare. Why is it when you see me in the coffee room you do not recognize me? Why is it when you look at me across the table, I am met with hardened eyes, reflecting a heart immune to emotion?* The anger bubbled over and I was faintly aware of him rambling on about types of chemotherapy drugs. I needed to focus. I needed to stop this spinning in my head so I could make a decision. I zoned in to the conversation. I heard myself asking for another opinion as his was not meeting my satisfaction. He agreed to consult with Henry Friedman at Duke University before deciding on the next step. Henry Friedman was the doctor of David Bailey who as previously mentioned had survived glioblastoma for twelve years. I figured Dr. Friedman was an expert on this type of tumour, so I wanted his input before deciding what type of chemotherapy treatment would be best.

The meeting continued with a discussion of the options available to us. One treatment involved stem cell transplants and platelet transfusions, which have horrible side effects and are very painful. Another alternative was not much better, consisting of three brutal chemotherapies: Carboplatin, Ifosfomide, and one other drug. Terry Fox was a famous Canadian athlete and cancer research activist who had had his leg amputated in 1977 after being diagnosed with Osteosarcoma. In 1980, with one leg amputated, he embarked on a cross-Canada run to raise money and awareness for cancer research. One of the drugs used in Terry Fox's treatment had been Ifosfomide. I was frustrated that a seemingly ineffective and outdated chemotherapy was still the drug of choice. For all the money that has gone into cancer research, why were doctors still using the same chemotherapy Terry Fox had used in 1977? Something seemed amiss. The cost of these harsh treatments seemed to outweigh any of the benefits. The third choice involved the use of a relatively new drug called Avastin, which had somewhat gentler side effects. The last recommendation seemed like the only option. After a panel of oncologists met for a consultation, they collectively agreed that two gentle chemotherapies, Avastin combined with VP-16, would be the best course of action.

The surgeons came in to see us the day after surgery. Both of them were warm and genuinely caring. One of the surgeons looked me in the eye with tears and said, "I'm sorry." The compassion in his eyes stirred me deeply. Softly, he said, "Your son, Zach, is very special. I've met very few people like him." His love felt like a warm blanket. He allowed his heart to be involved in his work without hiding behind professionalism. He had spent three hours trying to remove the scar tissue and tumour to improve my son's quality of life, and in spite of his efforts, he had not been successful. He grieved with us over our loss. He was sorry he could not do more, but it was not a cliché. He meant it. He genuinely allowed my Zach to enter into his heart, not just his head. He restored my hope that the medical system was not just made up of callous facts, charts, and procedures. There is a face behind each chart, with stories and dreams and hurts. To know the person and not just the disease brings the human side to medicine. Otherwise, it is just robotic, cold statistics that pour over wounded hearts like battery acid.

Currents of emotion left me struggling to draw a breath. This place felt empty, hollow, and void of any good thing. Too many appointments. Too many decisions. Too much crying in the night. Too much—it was all too much. The sounds of children screaming in pain and fear, beeping machines, interruptions at all hours of the day and night and the collective pain in that hospital added to my own already chaotic restlessness. The environment felt toxic, and the longer we stayed, the more poisonous it felt. God was hiding again.

It helped me to read another devotion from Ann Voskamp's *One Thousand Gifts: Reflections On Finding Everyday Graces,* and her words reflected like a mirror all that was within me:

No, God, we won't take what you give. No, God, Your plans are a gutted, bleeding mess, and I didn't sign up for this and You really thought

I'd go for this? No, God, this is ugly and this is a mess and can't you get anything right and just haul all this pain out of here and I'll take it from here, thanks. And God? Thanks for nothing."[3]

Her words echoed the variability of my emotional turmoil: peace one minute and dark anger the next. The Jekyll and Hyde of it all left me spinning, ungrounded and out of control. Brennan Manning calls this the "bundle of paradoxes,"[4] the believing and doubting, the love and the hate, the hope and the disappointment. Anxiousness, sadness, restlessness, and irritability became so intense I questioned whether there was anything in me unpolluted by pain. My bruised faith felt unwholesome and distorted. Pure joy did not exist in me anymore, only mangled bits of what used to be. I forgot what God's loving kindness looked like again. People would often marvel at my strength, but I was struck by how far from the truth their perceptions were. Most days I felt like Elijah, in the middle of the desert, "wanting in the worst way to be done with it all—to just die" (1 Kings 19:4 MSG).

Be strong and courageous. Do not be afraid; do not be discouraged, for the Lord your God will be with you wherever you go.

Joshua 1:9 (NIV)

CHAPTER 10

LIFE IN THE VALLEY

"Our life is a short time in expectation, a time in which sadness and joy kiss each other at every moment."

—Henry Nouwen

The valley was my home in this season. I had no way of replenishing all that was being drained out of me. A German word, "zerrissenheit,"[1] meaning torn-to-pieces-hood, describes the condition of my heart—shredded to pieces with constant bad news. Zach said I needed bigger sunglasses because I cried so much. That probably would have been a good idea. Days when I cried felt good, though, like I was grieving the way I should. Crying felt pure, unhindered by other emotions like anger and bitterness. C.S Lewis alludes to the strange comfort of grief: "I almost prefer the moments of agony. These are at least clean and honest."[2] In a twisted way, pain soothed, making memories more poignant and intimate. Pain reminded me how much I loved.

Two days after surgery, Zach's eyes were still swollen shut. Zach thought doing a few laps in the hallway might make the swelling go down and sure enough, it worked. After several laps of the ward, little slits began to open, and he could see again, meaning he would finally be able to watch *Lord of the Rings*. Just as he became engrossed in the movie, the therapist came in to teach him some relaxation strategies. Her unwanted interruption irritated him, but he hid it well, not wanting to hurt her feelings. She led him through different relaxation techniques, oblivious that he had one eye open watching his show. Finally she stood up to leave, and Zach smiled with his familiar tenderheartedness and said, "You are sure good at what you do. I feel so much better now." I thought, *Buddy, are you serious? You didn't hear a single word she said.* He honoured her even though he counted down the moments until she left.

The following day, Zach became obsessed with playing pool with Doug in the family recreation room. He would get up, play pool, and go back to the room, repeating this over and over again. It seemed unusual to me—like traits of OCD, an antidote for the swirling "what ifs" going on in his head. I wondered what it was like to be in his head. His brain was trying to compensate for the cutting and the growing tumour with parts of his mind dying and other parts regenerating. It must have been a battle zone in there, and he was trying to navigate his new reality, confused and frustrated that his mind did not work like before.

The sun streamed in through the hospital window, beckoning us to come out and enjoy its warmth, so Zach and I got a day pass and ventured out for a walk. He seemed unusually quiet and finally said, "Mom, I want to go back. I don't like the way I look." His words pierced my heart. We turned around and headed back, saying nothing. I sat with him on the side of his bed, looking at the deep scars in his head, thinking of the unspeakable pain he had been through, and hot tears came. Taking his hand, I reminded him that his scars were like those of Jesus: "Zach, God has chosen you, his most courageous warrior, to bring people to himself." Somehow this made sense to him. Perhaps this suffering had a redemptive purpose. I was reminded of Ann Voskamp's description of music being made in stress—as the string is pulled tight, "stressed and empty and stretched right out: this is the place of song."[3] I wondered if music would ever come from this pain. *Will we ever know pure joy uncontaminated by sorrow again?* I wondered.

Zach's muscles and joints were sore. His body ached from all the stress it had been under—too many pain medications, too much Decadron, too much constipation, and too much chemotherapy. His body balked at all the poison. Yet, in spite of the endless invasions on his body, ever so slowly, I began to see his strength returning along with his determination and even his sense of humour. He had seemed so downtrodden a few days after surgery, and I wondered if depression might be creeping in, but his joy seemed to be on the rise, and once again darkness was being pushed back. On the day we were released, our spirits soared at the thought of going home, seeing friends, and especially reconnecting with Carter. We could not get out of the hospital fast enough. On the drive back to Kamloops, I thought about Zach's thirteenth birthday coming up in two weeks. Memories of the past thirteen years swam before of me. Time had gone much too fast. Had I known I might only have thirteen years, I would have cherished every second. If only time could stand still. Silently, I sat in the car as emotions choked the life out of me. We were about to celebrate what could be his last birthday.

As his birthday approached, I posted on my blog that I wanted to do something incredible to commemorate Zach's entry into the teen years. Parents and kids from Zach's school came up with a plan immediately. On the day of his birthday, I dropped Zach off at school, delighted to see a little bounce in his step that was so familiar. It felt like an achingly long time since I had seen that kind of joy. It washed over me like healing water straight from heaven. Parents made sushi for his party—lots of it. This was to be his last birthday party, and the grade seven kids did an amazing job, throwing the best shindig ever! All the kids brought Legos for him. Zach felt covered in love and he came home beaming, knowing his friends cherished him and feeling thankful he could spend the next few days doing nothing but building Legos.

Even though his spirits seemed to be high, Zach's pain began to escalate. Along with pain in his joints and muscles, he started getting excruciating pain in his stomach and jaw. We increased his pain medications and his Decadron, but even then, he could not get comfortable. The tumour on the outside grew more each day, distorting his face dramatically. I could still see my Zach, but physically, he looked nothing like he used to. His face became more and more swollen, and the baseball-sized tumour was now an open sore needing dressing changes multiple times daily. He continued with chemotherapy and naturopathic treatments, but I knew we were losing ground. He deteriorated more and more each day. Shelley Ockenden, from nursing support services, phoned a week after we got home from BC Children's Hospital and left a voice message, explaining that she was part of the palliative care team that was to follow up with us. When I heard the message I slammed the phone down. I had no intention of calling anyone who wanted to talk about palliative care. My son had a lot of living to do, and this phone call felt like a death sentence. I planned to fast and pray until God gave me the healing miracle I pleaded for. I still believed God was going to heal Zach, and anyone who suggested otherwise got an earful.

Despite my longing for healing, Zach's cancer began to advance at a shocking rate. He regressed in age, acting more like a boy of five or six rather than a boy of thirteen. He wanted to hold my hand when we walked down the street like he did when he was little. Shelley suggested we read stories to him that we had read when he was small as a way of connecting. His favourite two stories were *Huggley's Big Mess* by Tedd Arnold and *Click, Clack, Moo, Cows that Type* by Doreen Cronin. Zach loved reminiscing over his favourite childhood stories and our times remembering and cuddling brought healing to all of us. Carter, too, enjoyed these times with Zach, laughing with him over their favourite stories. Zach's personality also changed dramatically. He began talking with strange accents and seemed to struggle more with social skills. I grieved over our loss as a whole throughout our journey, but I also grieved incrementally over the day-to-day losses. Each day we lost a little bit more of the Zach we knew.

In the middle of April, I knew it was time to talk with Carter and prepare him for Zach's death. My biggest nightmare could no longer be avoided. Doug and I sat on the couch with Carter and Saige one evening. My throat felt constricted and my stomach was nauseous. I opened *Gentle Willow*, the book I had read to the boys when Jay was dying. I hesitated before reading the words, wanting to prolong the truth for a little longer. My eyes blurred as I began to read the first page of *Gentle Willow*. I kept pausing to look at Carter, afraid of what I might see in his eyes. I did not see fear; I saw unbearable sadness. As I read this story that helps explain what happens as cancer or disease progresses, none of us could hold back our tears. In this story, Gentle Willow's friends notice her bark is lumpy and bumpy and her leaves are brown and droopy. Saddened to see her deteriorating, her friends try everything to make her well, but she continues to worsen. The animals sadly realize all they can do for Gentle Willow is give her a special medicine called love, tree sap to make her feel stronger and herbs to help her feel comfortable. Through simple explanations, the book helped Carter and Saige come to terms with what was happening. We talked about how they could love Zach in his dying and the importance of telling him all they wanted to tell him. The next day, Carter wanted to stop by the Christian bookstore on our way back from longboarding. He made a beeline for the Willow Tree sculptures. These sculptures capture moments in time and express love, closeness, healing, courage and hope. Carter chose to buy two Willow Tree sculptures, one of a little boy sitting down with his hand on his chin and one of a little boy holding a puppy. He wanted both of them, saying the first represented Zach and the second, him. Zach's sculpture was titled "Quiet strength, always there for me" and Carter's sculpture was titled "Above all, kindness." Carter wanted something concrete to show how death could not destroy the union between he and his brother. A few nights later, I found

Carter and Zach sharing chocolate chip cookies on his bed, both teary-eyed. I was not allowed in on their intimate conversation, but I knew they were making sure nothing was left unsaid.

Day in and day out, we had prayed for a miracle, only to find our prayers had landed on seemingly deaf ears. God had let me down. It seemed miracles were not in store for our family. I knew I had to make the dreaded call to Shelley. We arranged a time to get together and met for the first time in our living room. Shelley's loving, emotionally present way of handling our situation felt reassuring. She met us in our darkest hour without being afraid of our raw emotions. She introduced herself to our family, and with openness and vulnerability she began to ask the hard questions. I felt strongly that Zach needed to be involved in our conversation about his palliative care, and with the biggest ache in my heart I have ever known, I asked him if he wanted to be a part of our discussion. Courageously, he said yes. We promised him we were going to do everything we could to make sure he did not suffer and to make sure he died peacefully. I reminded him about how his dad had reached toward heaven during his last hours, probably reaching to the angels that would take him home. Zach liked that thought. He emphatically said he did not want to go to a hospital. He wanted to die at home. I assured him that I would do everything in my power to make sure that his request was honoured.

The not knowing was what scared Zach the most, but braving the dark places seemed to usher in the light. Once Zach knew the plan and embraced his freedom to choose how he wanted to live during his dying, he relaxed into the next stage of his life. I remembered how afraid he had been at five years of age when his dad had been dying. I sat him down and said, "Honey, Daddy is dying, and it is going to happen really soon, probably before you go into kindergarten." I had seen peace wash over him because this news got rid of the unknown. He found something to sink his teeth into. Similarly, he left the meeting with Shelley in control of the care process in his remaining days, and it helped alleviate his fear.

Palliative care can be difficult to navigate, but Shelley led us through, so our time could be freed to love rather than figure out all of the paperwork and nitty-gritty details of the medical system. We trusted her completely. She dropped all the professional jargon, hugging us, laughing with us, and playing with us. I knew Doug and I would not be able to manage all of Zach's care at home by ourselves, so I phoned Margie to see if she would come and be his at-home nurse. She responded without hesitation that she would come and stay with him until the end. With her nursing background in the ER, she would be perfectly qualified to do everything. Also, Zach and his auntie had a really special bond. They had spent many of his early years together. She had packed him on hiking trips, loved him when he fell and hurt himself, encouraged him when he was sad, and made him laugh with her endless silliness. They were two peas in a pod. I knew Zach would be comfortable with Margie at his side and she would know just what to do when he was afraid.

Margie loved without limits. She gave up her income to come and be with us. She put dressings on Zach's tumour, combed his hair to comfort him as she was giving him a needle, flawlessly delivered his pain meds, and told him funny stories to make him laugh. Zach's favourite way to pass time with Margie was by watching James Bond movies. Margie was aware of Zach's every need, and perfectly balanced his medications. She came with us to doctor's appointments, stepped in the breach if she thought something was not right, advocated for our family, phoned children's hospice in the middle of the night if she was not sure about something in particular, and sacrificially gave one hundred percent of herself not only to Zach, but to all of us. Margie reached up to heaven and brought down compassion and dedication, allowing Zach's final wish of dying at home to be a reality. My confidence in Margie's ability to care for Zach's medical needs freed me to be Zach's mom. The burden of figuring everything out was lifted so I could savour my last days with Zach.

All day long I walk around filled with grief.
A raging fever burns within me, and my health is broken.
I am exhausted and completely crushed.
My groans come from my anguished heart.

—Psalm 38:6-8 (NLT)

CHAPTER 11

SORROW UNENDING

"I hit a wall, a mountain falls on me. My stomach churns, wrenches. Every emotion collides, cascading, rolling, and finally avalanching into total panic. There are no tears. I am immobilized."

—Elizabeth Brown, *Surviving the Loss of a Child*

Millennium Falcon Star Wars Legos lay scattered over every inch of our living room floor. Doug and I had sorted the five thousand pieces to make it easier for Zach to complete his dream project. I found it astounding that a tumour could take over almost half of his brain, yet he could meticulously piece together such a complicated project. After about five weeks of building, Zach's multi-layered, intricately detailed space ship was finished. We lacquered it to ensure the pieces stayed in place. More than ever before, I was in awe of his commitment to persevere against all odds. People working for NASA would have found this Lego project challenging, yet my boy, who had regressed in so many areas, pressed through his challenges and triumphed.

Shortly after finishing his masterpiece, Zach began to deteriorate quickly. I felt imprisoned in a concrete wall of darkness as he slowly stopped eating and spent more and more time sleeping. He still loved his Blizzards, but he only got out of bed in the morning and evening to eat a small breakfast and dinner. My anguish over watching him quickly slip away moved like an animal inside me, predatory-like, paralyzing me with fear. To make Zach more comfortable, my mom and Ray had brought in an adjustable hospital bed with a memory foam mattress. That way, he could move his bed up or down easily as needed so he could rest more peacefully. He no longer had the strength to climb the stairs to his room, so he slept beside our bed in our room on the main floor. That way, Doug and I would be able to monitor all of his needs. In the mornings, I would wake up, listening to his slow breathing, knowing I needed to get up, but I was so grief-stricken I could hardly move. I wanted to bury myself deep under the covers and escape from each new day, as every morning, there seemed like no way through for my broken heart.

Zach had one foot in this world and one on the threshold of heaven. Mixed emotions swirled in my mind: I felt relief that soon he would be released from his suffering, and I felt devastation that I would never be able to hold, smell, touch, hear, or talk to my boy again on this side of heaven. I steeled myself to go on, to be fully alive in his dying so I could help him peacefully transition from this life to the next. I silently screamed, "*Defend us by your might, Lord!*" (Psalm 54:1). I poured out my heart to God, all of my bitterness, anger, sadness, and rage filling a pitcher to be emptied out before him. In pouring it out, a sliver of emotional and spiritual stability returned so I could make it through one more day. When I needed comfort most, friends began to send in their memories and thoughts of Zach. Here are just a few of the many beautiful thoughts people shared with us during his last days:

Zach, I was thinking about you today when I was trying to put my daughter Ainsley to sleep, remembering the times I left books from the library on your steps inside the townhouse in Gold River. Being your babysitter at the time, I knew your mom usually left the door unlocked in case she lost her keys. I remember reading to you from your giant book-shelf of books, trying to get you to go to sleep in your cool little bed. I am not sure if I ever divulged to your mom, but one night, after putting Carter to bed, I went to check on you . . . but there was no little boy in the car bed. I frantically looked around and just in time, saw you about to climb out the tiny window in your huge closet. You just looked at me and said, "Mocha, blankie, soother." You had thrown your teddy bear, blanket and soother out of your window onto the deck and were about to go adventuring after them. You were not too thrilled I had stopped you, but I was glad to still have a boy to read to the next day when, thankfully, I was allowed back to nanny!

Erika Annala

I took a walk on the trails yesterday and found myself praying for Zach. I felt a rising in me and prayed God would spare him. I shared with God how we had all learned so much from him already — "Wasn't that enough?" I stood in front of a newly blooming Saskatoon berry shrub. The flowers were so beautiful and fragrant and I picked one to smell. God seemed to be saying to me, "These are the most beautiful parts of the plant, but they do not last long. They die." My objections were qui-eted and I felt humbled. But God pressed on and I heard, "What happens when the flowers die?" I had to think a moment and then nodded, "Fruit appears."

Lana Langevin

Zach, I will never forget the moment I met you: on our front step. Bag of papers over your shoulder. Jostling about on your rollerblades. Sparkling eyes looking right into my soul. A confident and kind hand stretched out in front of you to greet me. "Hi! My name is Zach." And after that, well, we all know how it feels to be in the presence of Zach. I wanted to let you know how honoured I am to know you and that you will live forever in many hearts and souls. In our house, you left us all a gift — love, laughter and kindness. Thank you for passing some of your grace on to our boys, Adam and Finn. You will be missed in measures of enormous bike jumps.

Alan Vukusic

Zach, twenty-four youth, none you have ever met and many your own age heard some of your story as I read to them from your mom's journal. Everyone prayed aloud one after the other for you and your family. There was no one that stayed silent. Even those who do not yet know God the way you do raised their voices to him on your behalf. Perhaps because of your story some of these youth may come to know God the way you do.

Troy Grant

Zach, I never really got to know you well, but whenever I was around you I thought you were the most inspiring kid ever. When you came to youth, I knew you had cancer and I did not know what to think of it. But when you were hanging out and talking, I could see that nothing could bring you down. I could tell you were still a kid even though you had one of the worst cancers. You have totally inspired me to be radical for God and grow in my faith because your story is one of the greatest. I hope you know how much you mean to me and how much you have changed my life and others' lives. Thank you for being a great teacher.

Your friend, Ben Robertson

I don't know if you remember me, but I worked at the Summit location of Booster Juice. I gave Zach a gift card the day you and he came into the store. I tried so hard to not let him see me cry. I hope I was successful. I didn't really know Zach, but he completely changed my life. Every time you came into the store, he always had a smile on his face, which would put a smile on mine. He was so brave, so adorable, and without even saying much, he taught me how valuable and precious life is. I am not the praying type, but after finding out about his cancer, I prayed every night for him, so I consider him my own little miracle.

Sarah Boice

People's kind words felt like healing ointment for my soul. Zach's short life had transformed hearts of friends, acquaintances, and strangers alike.

As Zach's life slipped away, he surprised us with joy. In and out of consciousness, he smiled brightly when visitors came. He gave my mom the thumbs up when she went in to say her goodbyes. He put on his Jamaican hat and gave his brother the "shaka, shaka," the Hawaiian symbol of *aloha*, meaning everything is going to be all right. I smiled, pondering the beautiful ugly, the ugliness of cancer contrasted with the beauty of my triumphant son who bravely faced and conquered its viciousness. After being bedridden for days, he suddenly got the urge to jump out of his bed, run up the stairs and climb into his comfy bed with all his familiar things. He wanted to be in his own room one last time. I imagined him sitting on the floor playing Legos and drawing at his desk. I was aware of the papers, pencils, and art materials on his drawing table, still there from the last time he had sketched, and these items haunted me with thoughts of what would be no more. Zach, too, looked longingly at what he was leaving behind, knowing this was his last visit to his room.

On the evening of May 1st, I sat on his bed and asked him if he was ready to go to heaven. He smiled and said, "Yes. I am tired. I am ready to go." Calling deep on my courage, I held his hand and told him he could go to be with Jesus whenever he wanted; he did not have to hold on any longer. Jesus was preparing his beautiful place and sending the angels to come for him. He seemed peaceful, and said words that washed over me, sad and gentle all at once, "Mom, take really good care of Carter." His final thoughts were about his little brother. I promised him I would dedicate my life to caring for Carter, and with that, he fell back asleep. Carter sat by his bedside reading to him, pouring into his brother the beautiful medicine of love. As Zach became unresponsive, we continued to talk with him and gathered around his bed to worship. The fragrance of our worship rose up to heaven, and God released the angels who, no doubt, stood watch over his room, waiting for us to say our final good-byes before they took Zach to his eternal home.

One of God's finest was going home to the place I had told him about since he was a little boy. He knew without a doubt heaven had many adventures waiting just for him, and once he arrived, he would be instantly released into glory. At bedtime, we had often read stories about heaven, imagining what it would be like, enjoying testimonies about people dying, visiting heaven and then coming back to the earth. The four of us had read *90 Minutes in Heaven* by Don Piper, soaking in the descriptions of the "holy swoosh of wings," "the myriad of songs" from the heavenly choir and "the glorious hues and shimmering shades."[1] We had let our hearts soak in Jesus' promise: at the moment of death, the chains of this life will crash to the floor as we become fully healed, never to be sick or hurt or sad again. Zach knew the most ordinary moments in heaven would be greater than the most perfect moments on earth. We had daydreamed about what heaven would be like, and especially liked Randy Alcorn's description in his book *Heaven*, where he describes heaven to be like "sitting in front of the fire with family and friends, basking in the warmth, laughing uproariously, dreaming of the adventures to come — and then going out and living those adventures together. With no fear that life will ever end or that tragedy will descend like a dark cloud. With no fear that dreams will be shattered."[2] Because of Zach's confidence about where he was going, he felt the presence of peace in his dying.

I tucked in beside Zach for our last night together, and Margie slept beside me in Zach's hospital bed. Doug slept in another room because Margie needed to be near in case Zach experienced pain or other complications. At one point, Zach seized suddenly. Fear gripped hard around my throat, but my sister, calmly and with no hesitation, grabbed something out of her bag, injected the medicine, and he immediately stopped seizing and fell into peace once more. "Thank you, Jesus," I whispered, grateful he was not suffering. My anxiety was wild and out of control, so I had an Ativan to calm the crushing emotions that were taking me under. I could hear Zach's slow gurgling breathing beside me, each one threatening to be the last, and I breathed in rhythm with him and fell asleep until morning. When I woke up in the morning, Zach's body lay still and lifeless. Searing fear gripped me. I gently nudged him and whispered his name. Nothing. No pulse. I looked into his eyes, the rich brown staring lifelessly back at me. He was still warm. He looked like his eyes should come back to life and he should flash me one of his bright smiles, but he was gone. *Oh, God!* I could not believe I had fallen asleep and missed Zach's last breath and my last chance to whisper love into his heart.

The next thing I remember was when I went into Carter's room to tell him the news. I gently woke him, saying words I could not even believe were coming out of my mouth: "Carter, Zach died in the night." He shot up out of bed in disbelief. In his blue eyes were pools of incomprehension and despair. All he said was, "What?" Up until that moment, he had still hoped his brother would get well, but as reality set in, the news turned his world upside down. His big brother was gone forever. He no longer had his best friend to talk to, play with, or help him when he was struggling. The news was like steel wool to his heart. Meanwhile, Doug cried agonizing sobs in the bathroom, sounds I had never heard coming out of him. I hardly remember anything about the rest of the morning. The space between words with Carter and the arrival of staff from the funeral home to remove Zach's body are buried in a deep fog. Trauma stole my memories. When pain became too unbearable, my body compensated by stripping away memory. The depth of my sorrow released a psychological anesthetic to help me make it through. I do not remember if I touched Zach's hair, laid with him, or said anything to him—I know I probably did, but I do not remember. I must have cut his hair because I have some of it in a Ziploc bag. I would give anything to remember our last conversation together.

A stranger came into our room with a stretcher to remove Zach's body. The one memory I wish I could block froze into my mind with horrific vividness. I asked Carter if he wanted to watch as they loaded his brother's body into the van or if he wanted to be alone and away from the scariness. He wanted to watch, hanging onto his brother for as long as possible. Together, we stared out of the living room window, tides of fear sweeping over us, beyond words, as the van left the driveway with the body of the one we loved. Panic swallowed me up. Zach disappeared around the corner in a cold van with a stranger. Even though I knew he no longer inhabited his body, I could not stomach the thought of him lying alone in a funeral parlor. The thought repulsed me and made me frantic. I calculated in my mind that if I lived to ninety it would be fifty years before I would see my son again. *How can we go on in the void?* The question echoed through the depths of my being.

Shortly after the van backed out of the driveway, Carter looked at me with steely determination and said, "I want to go to my soccer game." His words surprised me. Going to a soccer game seemed like a strange response to this unspeakable loss. I was not sure what to make of it, but the look in his eye said it all — he was not negotiating. I realized his pain was calling forth his courage and perseverance. He had a mission he needed to accomplish. The ache of the loss sank deeply into his soul, and he needed to release it; he needed to play soccer to defy all that had just happened. Silently, we drove to the game. The team had a huddle, and coach Craig Berdusco got the kids fired up. The game was being played for Zach. Our family stood on the sidelines in awe, as endorphins, sadness, anger, and vengeance against cancer culminated, driving Carter to play the strongest game of his life. Nothing could stop him from scoring and dominating the entire game. He played his pain out.

Doug wanted to protect and guard his family against all the hurt death had left behind, so on our way home from the soccer game, he stopped to buy our long-awaited puppy that he had assured us he would never buy. He knew a puppy would not heal the wounds, but in a small way, having a bundle of playful life might make the long days ahead more bearable. During Doug and Zach's treatments, I had gone to the pet store with Saige to get some things for our gecko, Greeko, and while there, we had looked at puppies. As we watched them play, one of the workers had come by and asked if I wanted to hold one. Unable to resist, I pointed out a little black one. She was the only female in the litter and was the smallest. I had been drawn to her. As I nestled into her soft fur, she reminded me that something other than sharp bruising existed in the world. Saige tried convincing me to buy her then, assuring me Doug would *definitely* not be angry. I knew otherwise, so sadly I put her back in her kennel. But now, to my delight, my puppy was still there and, like a sign from God, she was fifty percent off. As soon as I picked her up, I felt fear subside. We quickly picked up all the things we would need and had her collar engraved with the hopeful name Carter chose: Lucky. Lucky seemed to sense we needed love after being in the battlefield for so long. She bounced with energy, made us laugh, and became healing salve during the dark days to come. Carter said her personality reminded him of Zach.

Along with Lucky's joy, two friends shared dreams of Zach they had experienced the night he had died. These dreams brought a lot of hope to our family. One of Doug's friends from the fire department, Dave Marcotte, dreamed Zach had died and was standing in a very peaceful place, when a man with a white robe walked toward him who looked just like Jay. His arms were open wide and he wrapped them around Zach in a soft embrace and whispered, "Let's go worship our Lord," and they walked hand in hand towards a bright light. My friend Lana Langevin, our family's greatest prayer intercessor, also had a dream the night Zach died. Lana had been burdened to pray for Zach, and during her prayer Zach had come to her, smiling his usual smile, without his tumour and said, "Hi, Lana. Thanks for praying for me. I am going to be with my dad, and he looks just like me." Anyone who knew Jay had known Zach was his son because they had looked so similar. I was thankful Jay had been in heaven when Zach arrived, welcoming him home. Although I knew once Zach was in the presence of Jesus all would be well, my earthly mind felt at ease knowing his dad was there to watch over him. Interestingly, Dave and Lana had their dreams at around the same time of night, very close to the time of Zach's death. Their dreams were gifts of reassurance to hush any doubts in my mind about Zach's safe arrival home.

Oh that I had wings like a dove; then I would fly away and rest!
I would fly far away to the quiet of the wilderness.
How quickly I would escape—far from this wild storm.

Psalm 55:6-8 (NLT)

CHAPTER 12

LAMENTATION

Just like Snow, sometimes grief comes one flake at a time.
Other times it comes like a blizzard. It melts away, but then
it always comes back.

—Julia Cook, author of *Grief Is Like A Snowflake*

After Zach's death, I began reading material from others who had lost children or other family members. I needed a road map to lead me through the searing emptiness. One of the hardest things to do is put pain into words. Books I found the most healing were C.S. Lewis' *A Grief Observed*, Gerald Sittser's *A Grace Disguised: How a Soul Grows Through Loss*, William Paul Young's *The Shack*, and Nicolas Wolterstorff's *Lament For A Son*. Others' experiences anchored me during the pinnacle of pain when I thought I was going crazy. The brave ones who had dared to write about their raw, honest descriptions of suffering after loss gave me the right to express and feel my own heartache.

The scariest part of grief is not knowing what to do with the intensity of it and not knowing whether the feelings are normal or not. At its worst, I can only liken it to what a psychotic breakdown must feel like. Only in reading others' experiences could I normalize what I was feeling. We live in a culture that expects people to get over things quickly. Our fast-paced world does not slow down for grief. After Zach died, grief felt like a lonely, isolating experience. I yearned to wail openly and express the deep wells of my pain physically. I craved an outlet for unspoken pain. My inward grief was terrifyingly loud, but outwardly it was silent. I felt compelled to keep my inner world hidden from the public eye. It took all of my energy to contain the wildness of it. I wanted to wear black all day, so people would know. I wanted permission to fall apart. When people asked how I was doing, I did not want to feel obligated to say I was fine to make them feel more comfortable. Wolterstorff's *Lament For a Son* in particular helped me feel freer to share my pain. When people ask Wolterstorff about himself, he shares the usual things people talk about in conversation, but he always tells them about the son he lost. He explains that his loss will forever be a part of his identity and he cannot and will not disown it. He calls his lament a love-song.[1] He helped shift my focus to the loving aspect of grief. Grief is not something to get over. It is intimate and entered into with courage. Losing anyone we love hurts beyond description, but losing a child takes pain past the threshold of tolerance.

Wolterstorff calls a child's death a "wrenching alteration of expectations."[2] A parent never expects to outlive his or her child. Since the moment of my children's conceptions, I carried an overwhelming desire to protect them. In my womb, they experienced how I lived my life, so I became overly concerned about eating well, getting lots of rest and exercise, and living peacefully so their lives inside of me would be enriching. I had wanted my babies to have the best of everything. After they were born, I watched them grow from being totally dependent on me to learning and discovering how to be their own people. I delighted in their joys and sorrowed in their pain. But now, my first-born was no more. Life was never meant to take place without Zach. I would never have the joy of watching him grow into a man. I thought about parents who have lost their children suddenly in traumatic accidents and have made the decision to donate their organs. Organ donation would be a way of keeping a part of them alive here on earth. Cancer robbed me even of that. I could not salvage any part of Zach's physical body because organs are not accepted from people who die of disease. I thought perhaps I would be able to cope if I knew someone had life because of Zach. I imagined his heart beating in someone. I thought of looking into his beautiful eyes again, even if those eyes belonged to somebody else. I longed for something tangible to touch and feel. My arms ached to feel him.

The unfairness of it all bounced around inside of me like shards of glass, cutting and abrasive, and I recognized the same pain in Carter. Doug and I grieved our son while Carter grieved his brother. No child should have to watch his brother die. One evening, I found Zach's bear, Mocha, on Carter's bed. Mocha had been Zach's favourite since he was born, and right up until his last breath, he held Mocha in his arms. Mocha had gone everywhere with Zach when he was little, and his old childhood friend brought him much comfort in his dying. As I kissed Carter good night, he put Mocha on his side table, fearful Zach's smell would go away if he slept with his treasured bear. Once his smell was gone, all that was tangible of Zach would disappear and Carter wanted to hang on to his presence. Another night, I went into Carter's room to take Lucky off his bed and put her in her kennel, and I noticed he was sleeping with all of Zach's necklaces on. His heart ached to be surrounded by Zach's things. Heavy-hearted, I went up to Zach's room, longing to be near him, too. I looked in Zach's closet at the clothes still in his laundry bucket. His favourite pair of pajamas and a few other things were tucked inside. I buckled under the sorrow. I never knew love could be large enough to hurt this much. The only way to make it through this season of heart pain was to join hands as a family and bleed together, each in our own way, but together.

Over three hundred people came to Zach's memorial service on May 15th, 2010. For my last birthday, Zach and Carter had given me a bright yellow pair of gumboots. When I wore them I felt so happy that I wanted to stop in the middle of the street and dance a jig. To honour Zach's fun spirit, I asked everyone coming to his funeral to wear bright-coloured gumboots during his memorial service. In the days leading up to his memorial, assorted boot vases with colourful flowers started arriving at our door from family and friends. Zach's funeral was filled with colour and full of life as everyone sang, worshipped, celebrated his life, and grieved his death. It is important to celebrate a life, but it is equally important to grieve a death. To celebrate without grieving diminishes the love, because grieving is a form of love. I soaked in the colourful sunflowers lining the stage, the memories of Zach's life, and the fragrance of worship, but at the same time my whole body throbbed with the merciless floodwaters of sorrow. When Zach's friend, Keegan Marchand, spoke about Zach, a dam of emotions burst within me. A twelve-year-old boy bravely stood in front of hundreds and spoke about his friend and his pain:

Zach and I met when we were eight years old in grade three. This is when Zach first started school at McGowan Park Elementary. We were in the same class for the next five years, and I have many good memories of our time together.

For one thing, Zach always had great birthday parties tubing up at Harper Mountain. It was such a blast running up the hill to the top and racing down on the tubes trying so hard to bang into each other! When I think back to our early elementary years, Zach and I played a lot with Legos at his house, and we swam a lot at my house. He seemed to have a passion for whatever he was doing at the moment. It didn't take me long to learn that Zach was always smiling. He was such a happy and enthusiastic friend!

Even in the past ten months since Zach was diagnosed with his cancer, he never lost his positive and fun-loving spirit. Because of his continued outgoing personality, I would never have guessed he wasn't one hundred percent.

In January, when Zach wasn't coming to school regularly anymore, he did manage to come to school for lunch to celebrate his birthday with our class. At that time, Zach was on quite a strict diet. So . . . for his birthday party, one of the moms made cupcakes for all of us and "special" ones for Zach. Zach's were made with artificial sugar and other healthy ingredients. There's no doubt that this mom went to a lot of trouble to make something healthy and appropriate for Zach. Well . . . I don't know how many people know this, but our teacher got mixed up and ended up giving Zach the wrong cupcakes. By the time she realized it, Zach was on his second cupcake saying, "Oh, these are *so* good!" Zach hadn't had sugary food for so long, no wonder they tasted so good. Our teacher was horrified, but what could she do? She just smiled politely and ended up choking down Zach's "healthy" cupcakes herself!

There's no doubt that in the last few months, one of Zach's greatest joys was food. You name it, he loved it: popcorn, ribs, and, of course, Dairy Queen Blizzards. I was lucky enough, along with some of our other friends, to have a couple of great sushi feasts with Zach. Most thirteen-year-olds would order the typical California rolls. Not Zach! The last time we went out for sushi, Zach ordered one of his favourite dishes that included eel. To be honest with you, the thought of eating eel did not appeal to me at all. When I asked Zach if eel was good, he said with his usual enthusiasm and excitement, "Oh, ya! It tastes like chicken . . . only a little chewier!" I'm not so sure about that but the next time I'm out for sushi, I'm going to try eel, just for you, Zach.

It is so hard to lose a friend like Zach. It is so hard because he was literally one of a kind. Zach was always smiling, right to the end. Zach was always so positive and polite. Zach never judged anyone, and everyone was his friend. Zach loved his life. Zach loved his family. He especially loved his little brother, Carter. Zach loved God. My life is so much richer because Zach was my friend. Zach is a true inspiration, and we should all try to live our lives the way Zach lived his.

I was so proud of Keegan. He had so much trouble not crying, yet he faced his sadness and shared his heart. His bravery gave me the courage to face my own pain. His stories about Zach brought back memories I had forgotten about and even in the midst of my unbearable sadness, I smiled as Keegan shared his recollections.

Shortly after Keegan's thoughts were shared, we watched a slide-show of Zach's life. As the pictures of his slideshow flashed memories of our lives together, I longed to sink into the pictures and relive moments in time: his arrival into the world, birthdays, and family vacations. The images soothed and hurt like salve and salt in wounds at the same time. I could not silence the deafening roar of grief. Like author Gerald Sittser during his season of grief, I felt "punished simply by being alive as tears turned to brine, to a bitter and burning sensation of loss that tears could no longer express."[3]

As we left the service, the emptiness suffocated. I did not have the energy to talk anymore. I felt smothered. *God, you need to pour your balm on my wounds. I feel like I am being buried alive.* He whispered back, "My grace will sustain you. I will not let you fall. Lean into me and soak in my strength." I felt I had experienced a second death. The farewell made it final. Zach was really gone. I did not grieve as one with no hope, but even so, Zach was gone. Once again, Wolterstorff put words to my grief-stricken mother's heart:

There is a hole in the world now. In the place where he was, there's now just nothing...there's nobody now who saw just what he saw, knows what he knew, remembers what he remembered, loves what he loved... Never again will anyone inhabit the world the way he did...The world is emptier. My son is gone. Only a hole remains, a void, a gap, never to be filled."[4]

When I closed my eyes, they ached from holding back tears and not having enough sleep. The past year had been one long, awful vision of hell and now we had to learn to claw our way out of its depths back into the land of the living. The living felt like too much work. To begin the climb from darkness back into the light felt like hiking Everest without oxygen support. Each slow agonizing step screamed at us to give up the fight. It was too much, too far, and the darkness was too thick. I was exhausted from trying to be normal, but my fatigue did not bring on sleep. I would fall asleep only to be jolted awake, gasping for air. All night long, I would drift off and then startle awake, panicked and confused. Even sleep brought no peace. I finally gave in to sleeping medication to ease the long, restless nights.

A few weeks after the funeral, the phone rang, snapping me out of my fog. It was the principal from McGowan Park School. The office had Zach's belongings and she wanted to know if she could drop off his things. She brought over his blue backpack with his lunch kit and school supplies, bits of loose paper and old Ziploc bags at the bottom. Sharp stabs of heartache made it difficult to breathe. Among Zach's things were his school files since kindergarten. As I leafed through his old report cards, something in me cracked. This pain did not feel normal. I was torn in two by feelings of longing and remorse. After grade seven, there would be no more report cards for Zach. This was the end of his life. The heartbreak surrounding me each day had no limits. Mother's Day came a week after Zach's death. Friends invited us to their place for lunch after church. Torn between needing to be alone and fear of being alone, our family decided to accept their offer. Moments after arriving at their house, I realized I had made a mistake. Seeing families together was like acid on my heart. Thankfully, having a puppy at home gave me an excuse to leave. I ran towards home, went into my garden, and exploded into tears. Reminders of Zach blindsided me each day. I would go into the garage to get something and see his white skate shoes on the rack, with his different coloured shoe strings still tied after our last walk together. I looked inside to see the outline of his feet on the insoles. Fresh dirt still lingered from only a few weeks before. I would look through the pockets of his coat to find Ziploc bags of pain medications. Every day the ache surpassed any emotion I had ever known. The only thing that got me through painful moments such as these were people's continued support on my blog, reminding me that they would never forget our son and his impact of their lives. Laurie Marchand, Keegan's mom, wrote about her son's tribute to Zach:

Today Keegan competed in the School District's Zone 1500m race. When the race began, Keegan took off like a bullet, I suppose to be in front of the other twenty or so runners. He sprinted so fast off the starting line, everyone in the stands (including me!) was sure he was going to crash and burn. Well, he continued to run very fast and after the first 400m, he was still in the lead. Another parent, who is a very experienced runner, yelled across the stands at me, "What is Keegan doing? He has come out way too fast!" I just knew he'd never be able to keep up the pace.

To the surprise of us all, he managed to continue this crazy pace and Keegan led the race to the end. He won his very first 1st place ribbon for the 1500m. His smile had never been so big. When I finally got to talk to him, I said, "Congratulations! Where did THAT come from?" This is what Keegan told me: "When I woke up this morning, I said to myself, "I'm going to win the race today . . . I'm going to win it for Zach." I cried. He smiled. He knew he had never run that fast in his life and he told me he had thought of Zach the entire way.

When Laurie told me what Keegan had done I wept happy tears. Knowing Keegan had poured out his heart for his friend soothed my soul. Like Carter, Keegan is a gifted athlete, so it made sense that both of them would honour Zach through their sports. In the same way Carter had dedicated his soccer game to his brother the day he died, Keegan had devoted his run to his friend.

Soon after Laurie told me about Keegan's race, a hurting man who attended our church wrote me a letter about how Zach's life brought him redemption:

At the Sunday service, the pastor sadly announced the passing of Zach. I overheard people talking about his faith and his love for God. They talked about his bravery as he battled cancer and shared about the love he had for his little brother, Carter. He touched everyone's life at church in one way or another. The pastor asked people to pray for your family and I found myself praying for the first time in twenty years. After hearing about Zach, I wanted to attend his funeral. On May 15, the day of his memorial, I listened to his friend Keegan tell his stories about Zach and I started to weep. I was a hardened man with no care for anything at the time — weeping? Zach saved my life and the lives of others. He inspired me to keep going to church and his story opened my eyes and softened my heart so I could see the truth. I now believe that "love bears all things, believes all things, hopes all things and endures all things." Today, I walk hand in hand with Christ and the dark thoughts and feelings I had are gone. Today, I am able to forgive so I can be healed. I look forward to meeting Zach in heaven so I can thank him for helping a broken man find God so I could have life again.

Anonymous

God's heart came through everyone's comments. People's hearts burned with love, broken people were being made whole, and lives were being transformed. The stamp of Isaiah 61 became the underlying theme of our family's story as God began to weave a beautiful tapestry out of our heartache. Strangely, our pain began to give off a sweet fragrance to the world. God held our tragedy in the palm of his hand, giving even our deepest suffering purpose. Knowing God was turning pain into beauty softened our sorrow slightly, but all too soon, sharp pangs of grief would send me back into the world of darkness again.

In June, Zach's school, McGowan Park Elementary, organized an assembly of remembrance for Zach, dedicating a bench in his honour. Doug and his friend Brent were invited to sing a worship song, and they chose Matt Redman's "Never Let Go." As they sang the lyrics, I sensed a deeper level of God's stirring. He was working life out of death. C.S. Lewis describes pain as a "megaphone to rouse a deaf world."[5] Could it be that Zach's story was a "ransom for many" (Matthew 20:28), a life radiating in the darkness to restore hope to those who had grown weary of life's trials? I saw foreshadows of this during his suffering, but in his death I felt the power of his story even more. God highlighted words from Brennan Manning's book *Patched Together* to me: "[Zach], for many years the people have forgotten, they have fallen asleep. Your pain and longing roused them, helped them to begin to remember something they lost along the way. Your journey and story have called them to life."[6]

After the song, Zach's teacher, Mrs. Oryschak, dedicated a trophy in Zach's honour to be awarded to any team winning the zone or city championship. The principal presented Zach's bench entitled "Praise You in this Storm" that would sit in the center courtyard of the school. We borrowed the phrase "praise you in this storm" from the band Casting Crowns because the lyrics perfectly described Zach's heart as he weathered the storms of suffering and death. Even after all he had been through, the raging storms, the loss of dreams, and the seeming absence of God's presence, he had still heard God whisper, "I am with you." Through it all, through every tear he had cried, God had held onto his hand and Zach had praised him in the storm. Zach left a legacy for his school, his friends, and even for strangers who heard about his story. God promised to make beauty out of ashes, and I could see him at work restoring all that had been stolen from us.

The grade seven year-end assembly at McGowan Park Elementary was possibly the most difficult thing for me to endure after Zach's death. The kindergarten class presented the grade seven students with roses commemorating their graduation to high school. As I looked at the little children, I realized how fast time had gone. It seemed like only a moment ago that I had held Zach's hand to take him to his first day of school. Zach, with his new school clothes, adorable toothless grin, and uncertainty about being away from home for the first time. He should have been going into grade eight with his whole life ahead of him, but as the grade sevens lined up to receive their roses, I scanned the line to the open spot where he should have been. The kids lined up in alphabetical order, so I knew when his name should have been called, but sadly it was not mentioned. In that moment, it was as though nobody remembered the awful void. He should have been there celebrating his achievements with his peers. He had gotten straight A's in spite of his treatments and surgeries and he deserved to be there, dressed up in a suit and tie, celebrating his accomplishments and his future. I wondered what it would be like to watch his friends grow up. My mind whirred. *Will I look at them and wonder if Zach would have been that tall? Will I always be making comparisons, trying to fill in the gaps of my missing memories? What will it be like to see all of them graduate from high school, head off to university, and find their way in the world?* I left the assembly sad and angry with all that would never be.

Like that hard day in June at Zach's school, the days and months after Zach's death brought landslides of sorrow. We lived in what authors Brent Curtis and John Eldredge describe as the "middle of a story that is sometimes wonderful, sometimes awful, [and] often a confusing mixture of both."[3] We had no idea how to find our way through our web of hurt. Everything we did reminded us of our loss. Memories lurked around every corner, ready to ambush us. When we went to Shuswap Lake during the summer after Zach's death, we remembered the times we had taken kayaks out to go cliff jumping and times we had pulled the boys behind the boat. We recollected warm summer days when Zach and Carter had played for endless hours in the water; moments when we had all been together. Now, the lake was not the same without Zach. Carter especially seemed lost. He did not know how to be in our family without his brother. Doug and I tried to fill in the gap by being extra playful, extra funny, and extra intentional about making sure his needs were met, but nothing could fill Zach's absence. None of us talked as much as Zach had, so the quietness became uncomfortable. Everything felt awkward and forced. Our family did not function well without our chatty, fun-loving Zach.

On our way home from Shuswap Lake, Carter said he felt sick. His grief made him feel physically unwell. People's grief often manifests in physical symptoms. For Carter, he felt perpetually sick to his stomach. His chronic stomachache was his body's way of complaining about the stress it had been required to contain. He had endured too many losses. In the same way Carter's grief presented in physical symptoms, Doug's did as well. Doug had begun to experience debilitating sciatic back pain three weeks before Zach died. Sometimes when emotional pain becomes unbearable, the mind compensates by reducing oxygen to certain parts of the body, diverting attention from the more intolerable pain of heartache.

We could not escape from the aftershock of trauma. Because Doug was in so much agony, he was still unable to take part in many of our family activities. While emotional and physical pain continued to lambast us, we received word that Maureen's cancer was worsening. Once again, dark clouds loomed over our family. We were suspended in one long painful story with no end in sight. Not surprisingly, Carter did not feel like praying at night. One night, when I asked him how God was helping him through his pain, he looked at me and said, "God has not done a thing to help me." My heart hurt for him. We all felt like Carter did some of the time. He just had the courage to say it out loud. His heart was ravaged, left broken open, hollow, and alone. He added God to his growing list of disappointments.

We were all disappointed with God and each of us grieved his silence and our trauma differently. As the darkness persisted, I wrote out pages and pages of longings and lamentations in my journal. I wanted to talk about my pain, whereas, Doug and Carter grieved silently, processing their sorrow internally rather than externally. Our grief was as different as our personalities. Sometimes my need to voice my emotions was overwhelming for Doug and Carter. They needed some distance from the intensity of our suffering. Their quieter way of grieving sometimes hurt my feelings. Demonstrative grief somehow seemed more appropriate to me. Each of us had to learn to appreciate and make room for our different ways of coping. I had to learn not to dump everything in my heart onto them, and they had to learn to talk about their pain a little bit more. We had to value the way each of us made it through each day.

I waited patiently for the Lord to help me, and he turned to me and heard my cry.

He lifted me out of the pit of despair, out of the mud and the mire.

He set my feet on solid ground and steadied me as I walked along.

Psalm 40:1-3 (NLT)

CHAPTER 13

AFTERMATH

"Loss presses us to see and feel in ways we hadn't previously considered. I want to put on track shoes and sprint in the opposite direction of loss, because it fractures dreams — but I must learn to lean into the pain and embrace it."

—Patsy Clairmont, *All Cracked Up: Experiencing God In the Broken Places*

While Doug needed time to rest his back, Carter and I needed to distance ourselves from all the reminders that brought the freshness of our loss back like a riptide. We made plans to visit Margie and Saige. We packed up our ski gear and bikes and headed to Canmore, Alberta, for some mountain biking and spring skiing at Sunshine Village in Banff. I felt overwhelmed with even the thought of packing, as my energy and motivation were at an all-time low. Depression threatened to take me under, but I thought if I kept moving, I could outrun it. We crammed our minivan with bikes, helmets, long boards, puppy supplies, and snacks and set out on our journey, glimmers of excitement rising out of the dead places inside of us. To our surprise, a small part of us was looking forward to something.

We stopped in Roger's Pass to take Lucky for a little hike along a trail called "Skunk Cabbage Boardwalk." The fresh mountain air soothed and renewed us all. We taught Lucky how to climb stairs and let her run like a little bear cub along the trails. For the first time in a long while, Carter and I felt somewhat free from cancer reminders, even if it was only a small, short-lived pocket of freedom. We arrived in Canmore that evening, had a quick visit with Margie and Saige to catch up, and then went to bed early, tired from driving all day. We woke up to sunny blue skies, coffee, and French toast, and we were excited about what our spring day of skiing had in store for us. The warm sun felt wholesome and the spring snow was perfect. However, once we were on the hill there was no respite for grief, even in an unfamiliar place. We kept having flashbacks of our times with Zach doing what he loved best: skiing. Out of habit, I would find myself looking for Zach on the slopes. Despite our hollow, dull aching, though, we still found inklings of joy in our environment and especially in the après ski volleyball game that we played in our ski boots. Over the next few days, Carter, Margie, Saige and I rode bikes along the Bow River, hiked local trails in Canmore and went for burgers at Eddie's Burger Bar in Banff, all activities that would typically bring our hearts alive. This time, though, our fun activities only highlighted Zach's absence. Our first trip without him burned holes of pain into our hearts. He would have loved every second of this excursion and it felt cruel to be enjoying it all without him. Survivor's guilt is a heavy shroud to carry. What right did we have to continue on without him? Carter's eyes held deep pain in them throughout the trip, reflecting the storm of grief he had endured over the past year. When I looked into his eyes, I felt an overwhelming sense of sorrow. Carter smiled, laughed and participated in activities, but like me, everything felt mechanical and void of meaning. I exaggerated joy that I did not feel in the hopes of seeing his eyes come to life, but in spite of my efforts he seemed lost in his own pain.

If it were not for Lucky, I am quite sure we would have turned around and gone home early. The emptiness outweighed the joy. Throughout the trip, though, Lucky reminded us of all that was good. We took her hiking with us and loved watching her learn to swim through streams, climb rocks, chase sticks, and hop over logs. Her joy imprinted hope on our hearts. On the drive home, I sadly realized our home no longer had laughter in it. I made a pact with myself that no matter how badly I felt, I would intentionally do things to resurrect joy. I would read funny books, put music on, and tell jokes even when I felt like pulling the covers over my head and sleeping all day. I would choose life, not death. My home would no longer feel like a morgue.

True to my vow, shortly after returning home, I made daily life-affirming decisions to offset the painful atmosphere in our home. I would bring in fresh-cut flowers from my garden. The bursts of colour would liven our spirits. I filled up birdfeeders so I could hear the joyful sounds of birds singing outside our windows. I began to list what I was grateful for:

1. Coffee and baked cookies
2. Wind on my face
3. The smell of fresh dirt in my garden
4. Solitude
5. The smell of fresh air on kids when they come in from playing
6. Blackbirds on bulrushes

Each day, I searched for beauty and wrote it down. I opened up the windows and allowed fresh air to ease out the stale reminders of death. I played worship music in the kitchen in the mornings, letting the promises of hope in the songs bring balm to our wounds. When nobody was home, I would go into my office and turn up the lively music of Jesse Cook and dance. Dancing automatically lightened my heavy heart. I hungered for dinner times to be filled with conversation. I was tired of the three of us staring off into space with nothing to say. The silence was deafening. I found Gary Chapman's *Love Talks: 101 Questions to Stimulate Interaction with Your Family,* and used it as a tool to encourage meaningful conversations. I felt protective of my family and did not want it to die along with Zach. Shortly after Zach died, Carter said Zach was the one who held our family together. More than anything, I feared our family would crumble without him. I wanted to assure Carter we would survive as a family no matter what.

A few weeks after we returned from Canmore, Doug and Carter made plans to visit Ryan, Kirsten, and Darcie, with the hopes of doing some skim boarding at Spanish Banks and taking in a Whitecaps and BC Lions game. There is nothing like a sports infusion to heal the heart. Meanwhile, I needed some time alone to process all the emotions building up in my heart. I wanted time to look through Zach's things and to feel his ashes without anyone being around. Once Doug and Carter headed off, I went up into Zach's room, touched his treasures, and opened his sachet of ashes. Mustering up courage, I touched the soft, white talc remains of my son, all that were left of his earthly body. I let the wailing and tears come. Alone, I could let go of all that was stuck inside of me. The hands that touched his ashes were the ones that had changed his diapers, cuddled him when he teethed, and soothed him from night terrors. I touched all that was left of the body of my larger-than-life, bright, loving, imaginative and energetic boy. Crying soon gave way to fatigue, and all I wanted to do was sleep. I looked at his picture on his wall, his brown eyes moving me to more tears. I basked in the comfort of them. If I stared at the picture and let my eyes relax, as you do when looking at an optical illusion, I could imagine he was really in the room. My eyes tricked me into seeing him in a three dimensional way. I ached to reach into the picture and touch his hair. Slowly, I made my way down the stairs, my body aching from sorrow. Grief literally caused my joints and muscles to hurt. I got into my flannel pajamas and cozied into my duvet. I thought of Zach's last night beside me in this bed and the loneliness consumed me. I curled into a ball and cried myself to sleep.

In July, our family began planning our trip to Kauai where we would spread Zach's ashes. Zach had wanted to go to Kauai for his wish trip, but the island was too far from a major center if something were to have gone wrong, so we had gone to Oahu instead. Now, we would honour his wish to go to Kauai. On December 12th, 2010, we boarded a plane in Vancouver. As the plane left the runway, I held onto Zach's picture and wept uncontrollably. Carter sat beside me, quiet, wondering at this outburst of tears. Despair fell on me like a thick, lead blanket, and I wondered if this trip had been a big mistake. It felt like I had forgotten Zach somewhere. I touched my necklace with Zach's fingerprint impression on it, studied the lines and contours of his unique design, and read the words etched in the back, "praise you in the storm." I wondered if the tears would ever stop. *Will this entire trip be tainted by sorrow?* We arrived at Lihue Airport late at night, rented a convertible Mustang, and made our way to a condo at Poipu Crater where we were meeting up with Darcie. By the time we arrived, it was close to midnight and we felt absolutely drained. After connecting with Darcie and sharing a glass of wine, we went to bed, eager to get an early start the next morning.

The next day, Doug and Darcie dropped Carter and me off at Brennecke Beach while they went into town to get groceries. We walked to the local surf shop, rented some fins and boogie boards, and made our way to the beach. The waves seemed gigantic to me, and as we swam out past the break, we got hammered as wave upon wave smashed into us, one after another with no space or time in between. Carter seemed to struggle less than I because he dove underneath the waves and then popped out the other side. My first attempt to duck under failed miserably because I forgot to push the front of my board down and got thrashed around like a rag doll. When we finally got out to the calmer, glassier waves, I felt like I had been in a marathon. We found it strange that we were the only boogie boarders out there. Surfers surrounded us on either side, but no one else was boogying. We caught a few waves in, and finally one of the surfers asked us if we would mind getting out of their way. Apparently, we were in the local "sweet spot," screwing up everybody's line. Embarrassed by our accidental breach of surfer etiquette, we made our way back to where the rest of the boogie boarders played. Carter caught on right away, but it took a few pile drives into the sand and many spin-cycle experiences before I got the hang of it. After getting groceries, Doug joined us as well. He boogie boarded like a champ, making it look as easy as riding a tricycle, although he held back a little because of his back and because he still had not fully recovered from his chemotherapy treatments. I enjoyed watching him have fun again. Many times during Doug's sickness I had been skeptical about whether he would ever be able to fully enjoy life again. Even though he was not completely recovered from the after effects of chemotherapy, he had been given a clean bill of health from doctors. He would need to have regular checkups for five years to keep an eye on things, but scans after his final chemotherapy and radiation treatments had shown he was cancer free. As I watched him play in the surf, I thanked God we still had Doug with us. I have no idea what we would have done if we had lost him, too.

The next day, Darcie wanted all of us to rent surfboards, so we rented some boards and went over to the gentle waves near the Sheraton Hotel. We flailed helplessly as each attempt to stand on our board ended in graceless wipeouts. Actually, Doug and I thrashed about, but Darcie and Carter finessed their way through the waves, making it look simple and fun. I am not overly fond of difficult learning curves, so it did not take long for Darcie and Carter's natural ability to get on my nerves. I did have a handicap to use as an excuse though. On our way to Kauai, when we had been at the airport in Vancouver, I had dislocated my shoulder in Starbucks. Because of multiple mountain bike crashes in my earlier years, I have very loose shoulders. All I had done was lean on the table in the wrong way, and it had popped out. As a result, I could only paddle with one arm, making it nearly impossible to catch a wave. Carter mercifully pushed me onto the waves so I could at least stand up on the board, if only for a few brief moments.

The next day we woke up to rain and wind. Carter and Darcie still wanted to surf, so we went to a surf shop to find out about some of the local spots that were good for beginners and intermediates. The surf shop owner gave us directions to "Infinity Beach," strapped our surfboards onto our Mustang (that happened to have cockroaches in between the seats), and sent us on our way. It seemed strange that nobody was surfing in this "popular spot" except for one fellow, who must have been as misinformed as us. The murky water, churned up from the night storm, looked less than inviting, so Doug and I opted out and went to a funky little restaurant to have a beer. Darcie and Carter played for hours, oblivious to the cold. When we returned the boards, the fellow asked us where we had been. We told him about "Infinity Beach", the muddy waters, and the strangeness of being the only ones surfing (except for one other guy). He furrowed his brow and looked at us like we were from another planet. "Well," he said, "The reason nobody else was there is because surfers never go out in muddy waters because sharks come in and feed in the shallows." His words left me speechless. Next to avalanches, sharks are my greatest fear. As I absorbed his jaw-dropping comment, he went on to say, "I told you that when I rented you the surfboards." In my head I was thinking, *Um, nope, I am pretty sure you neglected to tell us that because I miss a lot of things, but there is absolutely zero chance I would have missed that message.* I felt thankful Doug and I had chosen beer over surfing, eliminating even the remotest possibility of one of us being eaten by a shark.

During the evening, I pulled out our Frommer's guide to the best beaches in Kauai. The one that stood out to me the most was Anini Beach, described as being much like Tahiti. We all agreed that Anini Beach would be the perfect spot to spread Zach's ashes. Because the beach was surrounded by Hawaii's largest coral reef, it was protected from violent waves and was more tranquil than most of the beaches on the north shore. The calm, warm, crystal blue waters seemed like a perfect place to release Zach's ashes. On our way to the beach, we passed an enormous field of sunflowers, reminding me of Zach and confirming that we were headed to the right place. As we stepped out of the car, a light breeze came off the ocean, and the turquoise shades of blue-green from the water shimmered in the sun. We walked down the white, sandy beach and came to a tree that stretched out over the water, a perfect climbing tree. If Zach had been with us, he would have been drawn to it, climbing on it, hanging off it, and sitting in its branches, contemplating quietly. We all agreed this spot felt right. We read Zach's chapter, Isaiah 43, and then each of us took handfuls of his beautiful ashes and put some in the tree and some in the water. As the ashes sank into the blue, they shimmered gold in the sunlight. We prayed and then played in Zach's tree. Carter and Doug waded into the water to swim and came face to face with a sea turtle swimming peacefully near Zach's spot. The turtle looked at them, blinking, as if to say, "All is well." We had two confirmations that Zach approved of his special spot: the sunflowers and the sea turtle, two of his favourite things.

Sometimes I think tropical vacations are a shadow of what heaven is like. Long expanses of white beach, the scent of Plumeria mixed with the misty scent of salt water, fresh rains, and fresh fruit, all reminding me of eternity. I knew this was only a taste of heaven, but I could not help smiling, knowing how much this paled in comparison to what Zach was experiencing. We had the opportunity to hike sections of the Na Pali coast and take a catamaran up its meandering coastline. Velvet green pinnacles towered along the emerald shoreline, with waterfalls pouring into deep, narrow valleys. I cried, thinking this must be the closest thing on earth to heaven. My eyes were not accustomed to seeing this kind of beauty, and

I daydreamed of Eden. The majestic, all-consuming peace made me feel closer to God than I had felt in a long time. As the catamaran left Kalalau beach to head back to Hanelai, the sun's orangey, red bursts of colour melted into the sea. I was experiencing a piece of Zach's world.

We returned home to Kamloops feeling a greater sense of peace. I felt God had confirmed his love to our family, and I felt less abandoned and alone. Pain still dominated every waking moment, but somehow it felt less jagged and raw. I got busy detouring my pain. I coped with sadness by over- exercising and focusing on a cause to divert my attention from my grief. I did not see this way of dealing with my wounded heart as dysfunctional but, rather, necessary. Although I knew the only way through the dark valley was to go through it, I did not have the strength. Healing required taking "the road less travelled," but that road hurt too much. It was easier to appease my constant restlessness by exercising the pain away. In the *Shack Revisited,* author C. Baxter Kruger describes how grieving people often "medicate, go on autopilot, check out; or stay busy, get involved in a great cause, manage other people's inner worlds... or stay drunk in one way or another."[1] I was guilty of being the textbook avoidant griever. I coped by starting up my counselling practice to manage other people's suffering. Along with exercising and counselling, I also immersed myself in training for one of the toughest mountain bike stage races in the world, the TransRockies, in hopes of raising $50,000 for the Make-A-Wish Foundation.

My sister and I had agreed we would race the TransRockies as team "Zach Attack" (a name we borrowed from Carter's soccer team). Margie and I wanted to honour Zach and other children whose lives had been interrupted by cancer. Zach's wish trip had helped our family escape from our cancer world, and we wanted to give other children and families the same opportunity. The TransRockies follows a four-hundred-kilometre route across the top of the Canadian Rockies in the high alpine wilderness, through Kananaskis Country and across the Continental

Divide, with twelve thousand vertical meters of climbing. Margie had done the race nine times, but I had never done anything that closely resembled the kind of grit this race was going to require. I began training in January, seven months before the start date of August 6th, 2011. During the winter season, I went to spin classes, did circuit training at Aberdeen Judo Academy and ran with my dog. Most of the time I felt exhausted, but I preferred that to agitation and restlessness. In the spring, I started going on five-hour rides, some on the road and some on the trails. I found it difficult to motivate myself because most days I went alone. I would select my worship songs, and rain or shine, I would go out, determined to be fit enough to keep up with my sister who dominates every race she goes into.

We began organizing two fundraising events. One would take place before the TransRockies in Canmore, Alberta, and the other would be held after the race in Kamloops. Margie organized our first campaign at Sage Bistro in Canmore where we held a dinner and a silent auction, raising about $25,000. The highlight of our fundraising evening was when Uncle Shon started bidding on a signed Calgary Flames jersey. He allowed Carter to be his bidder and to Carter's delight, Shon kept giving him the thumbs up to bid higher. To everyone's surprise, especially Carter's, the jersey went to Shon for $20,000. His generosity reflected his love for Zach. I felt overwhelmed with gratitude and love as nurses, friends and family gathered to honour Zach and donate to a cause so close to our hearts. The place buzzed with joy and excitement as people mingled, danced, placed bids on silent auction items, and ate heartily. Both fundraisers, as well as the sale of "Zach Attack" jerseys, brought our total to $53,000, meaning five children would have their wishes granted.

As August approached, I slowed down my workouts, not wanting to overexert myself before the race. During my rest phase, I dislocated my shoulder twice, once skurfing and once doing a loose, rocky downhill ride with my friends—not ideal with only a week left before the race. Two days before the race, I loaded up my bike, my "enduro" supplements, my chamois cream for butt chafing, and my dog for the drive to Canmore. Once there, I would meet up with Margie and then we would head to Fernie where the race would start. The first of many glitches came when Lucky developed the worst case of diarrhea known in canine history. A friend had told me I should be feeding her raw bones so the amino acids would clean her teeth. Later, I found out dogs need to wean into this new diet, and bones should only be given to them for a few minutes at a time until their bodies adjust. I had let Lucky indulge on her tasty new treat, and did I ever pay the price! For two days, she needed my full attention, which kept me up into the wee hours of the night.

Although I was tired from my long night with Lucky, my nervousness kept me wide awake on the drive to Fernie. After a four-hour holdup due to a car accident, we finally rolled into Fernie. I felt tired and unbearably anxious about the next day. I breathed a sigh of relief when Doug and Carter showed up the next day. Their presence put me at ease. A few hours after Doug and Carter arrived, our support team pulled in. Rob Vecmanis, from the company that sponsored us, Wilson Mountain Sports in Lake Louise, volunteered to do our bike maintenance, and Anne Marie Fisher, a nurse from Banff, was our acupuncturist and massage therapist. These two gems worked tirelessly, not only by doing our bike mainte-nance and our massages, but by donating their time to other athletes in order to raise funds for Make-A-Wish. My mom, Ray, and Doug pro-vided all of our meals along the way and provided critical moral sup-port, letting me cry on their shoulders again and again on my low days. And of course we could count on Saige and Carter to cheer wildly when we crossed the finish line each day.

On race morning, Margie and I got up early for our 10 a.m. start, filled up our Camelbacks, put our layers of clothing in our packs, and did a short warm up ride around the block. I placed a picture of Zach and Carter on the outside of my pack and tucked some of Zach's ashes into my inside pouch. I wanted him near me for the whole journey. Our first stage was a thirty-two kilometre timed trial run to find our placement in the pack and to help reduce congestion. As the two of us waited for the starter pistol to go off, I felt like I was going to throw up all over the road. Anxiety ripped through my body as I had the sudden realization I could not back out now.

The first major hill climb was "Hyperventilation," which deserves its heinous name. We chugged up in granny gear, inching our way around the loose gravel switchbacks. My lungs burned, my legs throbbed, and my heart almost burst out of my chest. I had read about the trails online, and my first clue that this might possibly be the most gruelling experience of my life should have been the names of the trails: "Hyperextension," "Eco-terrorist," "Lactic Ridge," "Root Extension," and "Brokeback," just to name a few. The technical and gnarly descent through steep, loose, narrow shoots exhausted me as much as the uphill climb. My fantasy of having a break once we reached the summit died as I realized the down-hills required more concentration and more energy than the ascents. As we joined hands and crossed the finish line, I already dreaded the next day, a mass start with fifty-six kilometres of riding and two thousand meters of climbing. After a shower and some dinner, we headed to the awards ceremony, where, shockingly, we discovered we had come in second place. It felt rewarding to be on the podium with my sister, hon-ouring Zach.

After the first day, I found it impossible to understand why riders from all over the world voluntarily chose to do this race annually. I am not sure what makes people intentionally seek out pain. My only reasons were to pay tribute to Zach's overcoming spirit by overcoming some-thing arduous myself and to grant sick children their wishes. What Zach went through did not even come close to this, but at least I could know, if only faintly, what it feels like to want to give up, and to choose instead to press in, dig deep, and conjure up determination.

Since Margie and I had come in second in the time trial, we had to go to the front of the peloton, which terrified me. To be near the front of the pack amidst four hundred other riders was intimidating, to say the least, especially for a rookie who had no racing knowledge or experience. I am not aggressive by nature, but to position ourselves within the group, we could not be wishy-washy. We had to make quick decisions and adjustments according to others in the group. Typically, athletes in the front are in a more advantageous position for a number of reasons, including less injury due to crashes, less likelihood of being stuck in the crowd, and less energy spent manoeuvring around others. Margie knew when to stay back, when to pass, and which spots were safe to ride in. She pushed me to ride hard and be as close to the front as possible. Everyone jockeyed for position, and the stress of it all felt completely awful. I just wanted to blend in and go to the back where there was no pressure or tension. Each morning I dreaded the peloton more than anything else. I brooded over all the "what ifs." *What if I crash and take out other riders? What if I cannot take the stress anymore and have to quit? What if people yell at me because I am in their way?* Pressure mounted steadily each morning as I waited for the starter gun.

We raced for three days in the Elk Valley, enduring long days, relentless mud and roots, and highly changeable weather. We biked through excessive heat, rain, hail, sleet, and even snow. My face swelled, for whatever reason, and I had a difficult time eating. As soon as I put food in my mouth, I felt like vomiting. Even chewing food made me dry heave. Almost all of my calories came from a drink called Carbo-Pro (a mixture of complex carbohydrates), and Café Latte–flavored Perpetuem from Hammer Nutrition. At the end of the day, the only thing I felt like drinking was Guinness beer because it soothed my stomach and gave me the nutrients and vitamins I craved (Guinness beer is actually very nutrient dense).

Stage three of the TransRockies brought with it relentless heat and long hike-a-bikes that left me excessively fatigued. I kept dry heaving and felt cold, so Anne Marie set me up with an IV to help with the dehydration. In spite of everything, we held third place throughout, giving us an opportunity to speak about our cause and about Zach. The lead riders, Krista Turcasso and Angie Krasnay, traded jerseys with us; we got one of their lead jerseys and they got one of our Make-A-Wish jerseys. Krista and Angie were tough mountain bike competitors, but they were kind and compassionate, encouraging Margie and I every step of the way. I wanted one of their jerseys because I really admired them both and wanted something special of theirs to remember our time together. I also liked the flamboyant pink colour. We wanted to give them one of ours to show how much we appreciated their kindness. Zach Attack jerseys had become quite famous in the mountain bike race scene, many wearing Zach's jersey to show their love and support for our cause. Krista said our story empowered people during the challenging parts of the race. In a kind email she wrote, "The love and loss you shared about your son Zach truly touched us, and is part of our TransRockies story forever." I felt like our story softened the TransRockies in some way. It opened the door to compassion, kind words and positive attitudes on the racecourse.

Some of my lowest moments along the way were climbing heinous roads, wading through knee-deep mud mixed in with cow poop, and crossing the icy Elk River after a long ride through hail and rainstorms. My highs included marveling at the stunning views of the alpine, holding Margie's Camelback strap when I could not turn the cranks any longer, and crossing the finish line on our last day with my family cheering us on. On my two hardest days, I felt the presence of God and Zach. I prayed God would breathe strength into me, and I felt a gentle push on my back. At first, I thought Margie had her hand on my back gently nudging me along (which she often did), but I soon realized it was not a human hand urging me onwards. Three times I felt this invisible hand pushing me through the tough spots.

On day six of the race, I woke up thrashed. I could not imagine sitting in the saddle for five hours. We had to ride on an endless dirt road that just about killed me. Poor Margie had to deal with me crying, complaining, and hyperventilating. I secretly wished someone would run me over so I would have an excuse to quit. I did not want fatal injuries, just ones serious enough that I would be able to quit the race honourably. As I grumbled, a man came along, put his hand on my back and pushed me along the road. I wanted to jump off my bike and hug the life out of him. At the end of the seemingly endless road, he smiled at me and said, "That is just a little push from Zach," and with that he raced off.

Looking back, I find some moments on our journey hysterical. Retrospect ages humour well. As I mentioned, this race is routine for Margie—she takes part in many endurance races throughout the year, and, more times than not, she wins. She is an aggressive competitor, so I am certain my dramatic outbursts wore her down. She probably felt like putting in earplugs to drown out my incessant emotional breakdowns. I had a panic attack on the top of a trail called Jumping Pound Ridge and I felt like someone had squeezed the oxygen out of my lungs. I managed to wheeze out my plea, "Margie, I need to stop; I'm going to die." In one fluid motion, she grabbed my bike and started running with it, hers in one hand and mine in the other. I stared in disbelief, as she tirelessly bolted up the hill like she had been shot out of a cannon. What she did not understand was that I actually had to stop. I could not take another step, with or without my bike. I slowly made my way up the trail, crying and frustrated. Although Margie had exercised great patience, she had finally reached a point of exasperation. She handed me my bike with a look that said, "Hop on this beast and let's get moving! We do not have time for this hissy fit." Thankfully, she pushed me past my own limits, or I would still be riding the TransRockies, crying each pedal turn of the way.

On our last day, I fell into a boggy ditch while riding over a little bridge. I came up out of that muddy mess raging like a wild lunatic. I threw my bike down and had a full-blown tantrum. Margie got off of her bike and said, "Look at me. Focus! You need to pull yourself together. Get in the saddle, and ride. This is the last leg and we need to finish strong." She was right. Finally, we crossed the finish line in Canmore, greeted by newspaper reporters, Mom, Ray with a bottle of champagne, and Doug, Carter and Saige cheering wildly. It felt surreal that we had actually finished. My emotions reeled from fatigue to wild excitement about our accomplishment. I looked heavenward and breathed, "I did it, Zach." All the training, tears and overwhelming fatigue had been worth it for him.

That night, Margie and I got dressed up for the awards banquet, excited to wear something other than our biking attire, and even more excited about eating a truckload of food. As soon as the race ended, my typical, ferocious appetite came back, and I could not wait to eat all the food I had not been able to for the past week. We took the podium that night as third place finishers, awarded with many prizes, including a free entry for the 2012 TransRockies (as if I would be using that!) Without Margie pushing me past my breaking point, I would not have accomplished my goal. Because of her love for Zach and her love for mountain biking, she pressed in when I was not able to find the strength within myself, encouraging me and inspiring me to higher levels of excellence.

My whole TransRockies experience reminded me of my grief journey. Each day had been a marathon. Unforeseen obstacles often left me in such despair I did not think I would ever finish the race. So many days I felt hope draining out of my spirit. I had started the race full of energy and enthusiasm, but not too far in, I realized the race was not what I thought it would be. Around each twist and turn in the road there was a false summit. I would think I was almost at the end when suddenly it would start to storm and there would be a heinous climb ahead that seemed unconquerable. I would gather all the strength I had in me for that one climb, but when I got to the top, there was another climb worse than the one before. This went on for seven days. Each morning, panic and fear welled up in me as I contemplated what I would be required to overcome next. I felt paralyzed when my imagination would get the better of me and I feared that what lay ahead would be worse that what I had already endured. Some days it was the flat, dirt roads that seemed more unendurable than the steep, intense single track climbs. The boring plodding on for long hours was agonizing. All of my energy was swallowed up as I wondered, *how long will this long road continue before something changes?* Miles of road stretched out before me with no finish line in sight.

Grief, too, had many false summits. Just when I thought I might be making progress in my pain journey, I would come to an impassible wall. The dark storm clouds would roll in and cover the sun. My emotional pain was fierce and untamed and stopped me in my tracks. I was unable to take steps forward. In fact, it seemed I was going backwards. Any progress I had made was lost as ambushes of regret and fear pressed up against me. I would look at the long road ahead and fall to my knees in hopelessness. There was no way through. I could not make it up the mountain of heartache because I was certain when I got to the top, there would be another hill, and likely it would be more treacherous then the last one. Or worse, maybe a flat long road of lifelessness loomed ahead with no twists and turns—just a flat, unexciting road with no change. The same feelings of emptiness would plague me day in and day out.

In my spiritual journey and in the TransRockies there was always the temptation to give up before getting to the finish line. The long road ahead took more energy than I had, yet in my heart I hoped some of my pain might be worth it if I was able to see from a mountaintop perspective. There, I would be able to look down on all I had endured along the way and see beauty in the most painful places. But to get to the top of the mountain, I needed to step into the footsteps of Jesus. I remember when I was a little girl, my dad would carve footsteps into the steep slopes so I could step into his steps and not slip or fall. Likewise, when we are faced with impossible hurdles, Jesus gently reminds us to step into his footsteps so the climb is not so strenuous. He shows us the way out of the valley so we can finish the race well.

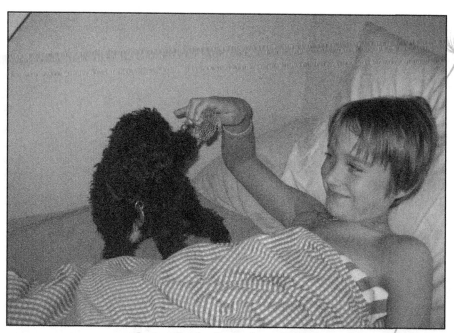

Carter, Greeko the Gecko and Lucky

Stage four of the TransRockies, about to cross Elk River after a day of hail, sleet, and mud

Crossing the Elk River, praying I don't slip or lose my bike

Finally, after seven days of blood, sweat, and tears we crossed the finish line in Canmore, Alberta

Sunflowers reminding us of Zach as we drove to Anini Beach to spread his ashes

Darcie playing in Zach's tree at Anini Beach

Beautiful Anini Beach

Carter spreading Zach's ashes

He will wipe away every tear from their eyes, and there will be no more death, sadness, crying, or pain, because all the old ways are gone.

Revelation 21:4 (NCV)

CHAPTER 14

BEAUTIFUL THINGS OUT OF THE DUST

"We are torn loose from earthly attachments and ambitions. And we are quickened to a divine but painful concern for this world. He hurls the world into our hearts, where we and He together carry it in infinitely tender love."

—Thomas R. Kelly

Even though we tried to soak up every last drop of joy in the middle of our pain, our lives continued to take us on unwanted detours. Maureen's health continued to decline. She began to have trouble breathing and talking as her lungs filled with fluid. The darkness of death was back haunting us while hurting and stealing Maureen's life. I hated cancer's presence, always looming, threatening, and devouring. It seemed to attack the ones with the kindest hearts. Maureen's joy had always been infectious. She made her grandkids feel like nothing in the world mattered more to her than them. She had always loved having

them for sleepovers over the years. Together, they had baked chocolate chip cookies (which her grandkids would eat faster than she could
make) and snuggled together in cozy blankets watching movies. During
the days, she took them geocaching, using her GPS to hide and seek
little containers called caches that had little trinkets or small toys tucked
inside. She delighted in what her grandkids delighted in and cared about
even the smallest details of their lives. And now, we were losing her. I
could not imagine how we would recover without Maureen in our lives.

On a cold afternoon in the middle of January 2012, I headed to
Maureen's place, looking forward to our usual conversations about life
over a hot cup of tea. She greeted me with an enthusiastic hello, and in
spite of her walker and her laboured breathing, she prepared us a cup
of tea. She loved to serve, so I did not want to step in and take over the
role she loved, but I could tell she was not doing well. We sat across from
each other at the table and, as usual, she lovingly asked how all of us
were doing. I had trouble concentrating because I could tell something
was wrong. We talked a little while longer until I finally asked her if she
thought we should go to the emergency room at the hospital. She hesitantly agreed to go. After hours and hours of waiting together, Maureen
was finally admitted so the doctor could drain fluid from her lungs. After
that, every two days her lungs would fill up again, so Maureen made the
decision to go into hospice where she could have around-the-clock care.

During Maureen's time at Marjorie Snowden Hospice, her family
gathered around, bringing her much peace and comfort. As soon as
Carter got home from school, he would grab his BMX bike and ride down
to visit her. She cherished her remaining days with family. With her usual
optimistic attitude, she told us hospice felt like a retreat. She is probably
the only person to have framed palliative care in such a light. I had a difficult time going to visit her. I only went a few times a week because the
injustice of it all broke me. I found myself withdrawing from her dying.
I did not want to face her suffering when the pain of losing Zach still felt

so raw. I marvelled at Carter's courage to visit her so often. During her last days, I sat by her bed and read Psalm 23, her favourite Bible chapter:

The Lord is my shepherd; I have everything I need. He lets me rest in green meadows; He leads me beside peaceful streams. He renews my strength. He guides me along right paths, bringing honour to his name. Even when I walk through the dark valley of death, I will not be afraid, for you are close beside me. Your rod and your staff protect and comfort me. You prepare a feast for me in the presence of my enemies. You welcome me as a guest, anointing my head with oil. My cup overflows with blessings. Surely your goodness and unfailing love will pursue me all the days of my life, and I will live in the house of the Lord forever (Psalm 23: 1–6).

Carter read the same verse to her when he went to visit, loving her the way he had loved his brother in his dying. I believe both of my boys inherited their courage from King Jesus and from their Grandma Laird. As I watched Maureen breathe her last breath, I thought of how much her dying looked like Zach's had, peaceful and painless. Carter had made the decision not to come during Maureen's last few hours. He knew what he needed—he had said his goodbyes and wanted to remember his last moments with Maureen without the taint of death. On March 16th, 2012, Maureen died.

The steady seepage of grief had been so constant in our lives that it almost felt normal. I looked at all of us crowded into Maureen's room: Maureen's brother, John, and her sister, Anne, her mother, Joan, Grandpa Skye, her daughter, Willow, her son-in-law, Taylor, and her grandson, Carson. Collectively we were losing a sister, daughter, mother, grandmother, and wife. Once again, the tide of sorrow rolled in, and we were left trying to make sense of our worlds without another one we loved. It seemed as though there was no way to escape the path of dark disease and broken dreams that defined our lives. The void was immeasurable and unfathomable. In the days following Maureen's death, I ran around doing endless, unnecessary tasks: cleaning, straightening and obsessing about irrelevant details as a way to self-soothe. Gerald Sittser, after the loss of his family in a car accident, said tragedies can be a "very bad chapter in a very good book."[1] At this point in time, though, all I could see was the cruel ending of this chapter. I could not see any good thing coming out of all this death.

Shortly after Maureen's passing, Doug's worship band, "One Silver Coin," was scheduled to play at a local bible study. I was not sure whether or not I wanted to go, but eventually decided I would go to support Doug. Once there, my reluctance lifted and I was caught up in the atmosphere of worship. I began weeping, overwhelmed by the love of God. Katherine Murray, a woman who was scheduled to preach that evening, was lying face down on the floor throughout worship. I wondered if I would ever be in such an intimate place with God. After the band finished, Katherine made her way to the front to speak, but paused before starting, connecting with God. She announced she was "kyboshing" the teaching she had planned to share because she felt God was doing something else. She then began to describe the pain of my own heart in vivid detail. She said she sensed someone had experienced tremendous pain and was overcome with doubt about whether God actually cared or noticed. She continued to describe the clouds of sorrow looming over me. Tears streamed down my face as a knowing began to take root in my heart: God really did love me and my pain was not invisible to him. I knew this in my head, but my heart was hounded with doubt. I believed God was singling me out so he could show me his deep compassion.

Afterwards, she called people forward for prayer. Too nervous to go to the front, I asked God to bring Katherine to me and within moments, she began making her way toward me. She hesitantly sat down, promising me she was not trying to scare me and then she said, "God shone a light on you as if you were the only one in this place. His heart is bent toward you." She told me God had a verse for me, and she shared the same one

Pastor Lamont had shared with me so many years before when Jay was dying: "He will shield you with his wings. He will shelter you with his feathers. His faithful promises are your armor and protection" (Psalm 91: 3–4). God knew how much that verse meant to me and he wanted to assure me of his love. Katherine sensed God was lifting the dark layers of grief so I could experience the sunlight of his love again. Before she got up to leave, she handed me her phone number. She thought God wanted her and I to connect beyond this meeting. Months went by before I found the tiny piece of paper she had scribbled her phone number on. Mustering up courage, I phoned her. That call changed my life and my relationship with God.

In spite of my special encounter with God, my spirit still felt heavy inside of me. One minute I would be weeping, and the next I would be filled with anger. Anxiety interfered with my daily life. I would go to the grocery store, forget what I had gone for and panic, feeling overwhelmingly disoriented. My emotions were hazy. I felt cheated by life and resentful toward people who still had what I had lost. My actions were detached from my thoughts and feelings, and I felt confused by warring emotions that would change minute by minute. The most unsettling emotion of all was the feeling of nothingness. I was often numb and I did not care about anything. Any attempt to feel was too raw and the emotions too brutal, so I pushed them away and locked the door of my heart. This did not look like grief; rather, it looked like guilt, anxiety, irritability, and hypersensitivity to noise or chaos of any kind. I needed help!

Katherine and I set up an inner healing session after chatting over tea in my garden. Katherine shared that an inner healing session would gently peel back pain layers so wounds could be healed. She talked about God's promise to us that his children can hear his voice when their hearts are open and quiet before him. One of the ways we can perceive God's love for us is through our imagination. God used his imagination when he created the world, unfolding a beautiful feast for our senses.

God first imagined colourful sunsets, majestic mountains, autumn leaves with bursts of colour, and intricate, carefully crafted designs on seashells. Then he spoke them into being, putting physical form to the pictures in his mind's eye. Because we are created in God's likeness, we too can use the imaginations he has given us to connect with him and sense his compassion for us. When King David talked about God "leading him beside still waters" in Psalm 23, for example, he was making a heart connection with God in a meditative way. When we commune with God in this way, our hearts become fully alive and we can be deeply moved. Truth moves from our heads down to our hearts. During this intimate time with God, we can ask him questions and be still to hear what he shares. In his loving kindness, he often takes us to the wounded places in our heart he wants to restore. Sometimes, what he shares with us comes through a gentle knowing in our hearts and other times it is more obvious, coming in detailed pictures or words. How he speaks to each person is different, but his ways are always loving and never condemning.

As Katherine shared the process of inner healing with me, I realized our sessions together would be much more than behavior modification and coping strategies. Inner healing would involve a heart transformation. I was somewhat uneasy about our first session, but also relieved I was finally taking a concrete step toward getting well. Laying my heart out for God to heal felt risky and inviting all at the same time. I was really nervous at first, afraid I might not "do it" right, or worse, that I might not see or hear anything from God.

When I arrived for my session, Katherine and Danielle McClurg (who would be recording the session) met me in a cozy room that felt safe. Katherine and Danielle's warmth put me at ease. They played some worship music and nervousness gave way to feelings of peace and comfort. Katherine asked Jesus some questions and he began to speak to my heart in pictures. Her first question was about where Jesus wanted to meet with me. Almost instantly, I saw Jesus and I sitting on a log beside a pool of water. He was smiling at me, assuring me it was safe to ask him any-thing. She then asked him what aspect of his nature he wanted to reveal to me. In my mind I saw a lion and a lamb. He wanted me to know he was fighting for me and protecting me, but he also wanted me to know he was tender, nurturing and safe. Finally, she asked Jesus what he wanted to talk to me about. At this point, Jesus directed me to the unhealed parts of my heart. Trusting him, I shared my hurts with him: my regrets as a mom, my pain about falling asleep before Zach died and my anger that wounded people in my family. Katherine then asked Jesus to bring all of my emotions and pain into his light so he could bind up my wounds. Soon, a picture formed in my mind of a pool. Jesus was in the pool and as I joined him, he started pouring water over my head. He was washing away the pain, refreshing me and making me new. He was giving me a fresh start. He promised me I could come back to the pool anytime I needed cleansing and refreshing.

The process of inner healing felt beautiful and gut wrenching at the same time. Katherine said I filled the garbage can with more Kleenex than anyone she had ever done an inner healing session with before. We met several more times, and each time Jesus took my healing to a new and deeper level. In one of the sessions, I had a vivid image in my mind of being sick. Jesus came and tucked me into bed, put warm cloths on my forehead, and lovingly sat with me, stroking my hair and nursing me back to health. He whispered, "You have been a loyal and loving care-giver. Let me nurse you back to health." Another profound turnaround for me in my healing came during one of my personal quiet times when I asked Jesus where he had been when Zach lay in his hospital bed after his craniotomy. Immediately, he took me to the garden of Gethsemane, where he had cried tears of blood during his darkest hour here on earth. In my heart I heard him say, "During my deepest time of anguish before I went to the cross — that is the same pain I felt as I sat with Zach in that hospital room." Immediately, I fell in love with the one who knew my pain intimately because he had experienced it in his own body and in his own emotions. His heart broke with my heart. I felt able to re-connect with him again, and the gap between us began to close. The roots dark-ness had entangled me with, all the lies and unresolved pain, began to loosen their hold on my soul.

From our inner healing sessions, I learned a process of connecting with Jesus that has been invaluable to me. Most days, I spend time lis-tening to worship music so his love can wash over me. Next, I ask Jesus to create in my mind a safe place where we can talk about things on my heart and on his heart. Most often our meeting place is an imaginary one. Quite often it will be a cabin, a place by a quiet stream or on a beach. There, when my senses are fully alive, I can rest in our special place and allow his love to wash over me. After "soaking" for a while, I then ask him questions and journal his responses. Many of the heart questions I ask him are borrowed from questions Eden and Brad Jersak recorded in their book, *Rivers From Eden*, such as:

> *Jesus, where can we meet together?*
> *What dreams do you want to awaken in me?*
> *What burdens will you carry for me?*
> *What promise do you have for me today?*
> *What in me causes you grief? Joy?*
> *Do you have a gift for me today?*
> *What gift can I offer you today?*
> *What is on your heart, God?*
> *Who am I to you?*
> *God, can you tell me what you are like?*
> *Can you show me what wounds you want to heal today?*[2]

By communing with God this way, I was able to discern his heart for me when life was hard. He brought fresh hope to my day-to-day experiences because I realized he truly was my best friend. His unfailing love made each day one to be treasured instead of one to be plowed through. Asking God questions and being still enough to hear his answers was my portal out of the valley of suffering.

As months passed, God's compassion melted away the sharp edges of my grief during these contemplative times. The shadows became grey instead of black, and Hope himself gave me a reason to live. God tugged at my heartstrings and encouraged me to dream again and trust him with my heart's desires. I read Mark Batterson's book *Circle Maker* and began circling promises in my Bible God had for my family. Then I spoke those promises out loud as blessings. A better story began to emerge as God strengthened me with his love. Now, God's loving kindness propelled me to care for others in pain the way he had cared for me. He asked me, "Are you willing to take this tragedy and point people toward my love? Will you be the one to rescue lives that have lost all hope? Will pain attune your heart to the suffering in the world?" I jumped up and responded, "Yes, Lord. I will do it! I will allow you to rewrite this tragedy so people in pain can find you and have abundant life. I circled Isaiah 61 as my special chapter:

> "The Spirit of the Sovereign Lord is upon me, because the Lord has appointed me to bring good news to the poor. He has sent me to comfort the brokenhearted and to announce that captives will be released and prisoners will be freed. He has sent me to tell those who mourn that the time of the LORD has come, and with it, the day of God's anger against their enemies. To all who mourn . . . he will give beauty for ashes, joy instead of mourning, and praise instead of despair. For the LORD has planted them like strong and graceful oaks for his glory" (Isaiah 61:1–3).

As I meditated on this chapter, God began to unfold his plans for me and I recorded his words over my life in my journal:

Dana, I have given you a special task. You have been longing for joy for a long time. You have been hungry to see more of my goodness, and I want to give you the desires of your heart. I have chosen you to bring good news to those who have been waiting for God to act in their midst. I have set you apart to bring good news to the poor in spirit and to heal those broken in heart, especially to heal the ones who have misunderstood who I really am. I will give you a bouquet of roses for ashes. Like an oak tree, you have weathered many storms. Your roots are very strong. You have been bombarded with pain and sorrow, but renewal is on the way and your spirit will be awakened like never before. You will be fully alive. You will sing and dance with happiness.

God showed me that our family's story and testimony were keys to somebody else's freedom. Our story had the potential to monumentally influence how God was carrying out his plans in other people's lives. I felt like Zach and all of heaven were shouting, "Make it count! Make this story one of hope, freedom, and love." Without pain, I do not think I would have such a passion to love others as Christ has loved me.

As long as I remained in trauma, I had a hard time seeing who Jesus truly was. In the Bible, Jesus' disciples walk with him on the dusty roads day in and day out, watching him do miracles of love every day. Yet, after his death, they are not aware of his presence when he starts walking down the road with them (Luke 24:13). The reason they cannot recognize him is because they are so full of sorrow after his death. Trauma blinds them. C. S. Lewis writes about how we "can't see anything properly while [our] eyes are blurred with tears."[3] However, when Jesus heals trauma, we can see his purposes clearly again. We can see who he really is. When he takes mortar from heaven and heals the cracks of our broken dreams, love starts to grow and expand until it spills out to others around us. As I found my way into healing, I began to thirst for fresh insight and fresh purpose. Grief can be a very self-focused journey, but my heart began to burn for the greater purposes of love God had for me. I wanted to use my pain to heal others.

See, I am doing a new thing! Now it springs up; do you not perceive it?
I am making a way in the wilderness and streams in the wasteland.

Isaiah 43:19 (NIV)

CHAPTER 15

NAKURU, KENYA

I grasped the meaning of the greatest secret that human poetry and human thought and belief have to impart: the salvation of [people] is through love and in love."

— Viktor Frankl

Even though I was experiencing a lot of healing with meditative prayer, I still felt there was a block between God and myself. I continued to waver between pulling away from God and drawing near to him. I was discouraged when my prayers still felt habitual rather than heartfelt. I hungered for something tangible from heaven to heal my bruised faith. Blind faith felt exhausting. I wanted to see miracles for myself. Often when I am having trouble hearing God's voice, I will go for long runs in nature, where I can shut off my intellectual mind so it does not interfere with my heart connection with God. Hungry to hear from Jesus, I laced up my running shoes on a hot July afternoon and headed into the trails in Peterson Creek. Worship music about God's miracles began stirring my heart and God spoke to me through these songs. With each step I took, I became more and more excited. I sensed God saying, "I am doing a new thing. You will see the miracles you have longed for. There is a time for everything, and a season for every activity under heaven . . . a time to weep and a time to laugh, a time to mourn and a time to dance . . . your season for dancing has come. You have endured the weeping season." My spirit quickened within me and I felt the presence and warmth of God's love.

Shortly after God gave me this promise, Katherine told me that Steve Stewart from Impact Nations was scheduled to speak at the Kamloops Vineyard Church. He would be sharing the miracles his short-term missions' teams were seeing all over the world. Impact Nations ministers in Haiti, Nicaragua, Uganda, Kenya, and the Philippines and has a mandate to go to the "most vulnerable in the developing world with a message of hope along with practical and supernatural expressions of God's compassion and power."[1] Impact Nations brings sanitation education, medical clinics, water programs, and feeding programs to those living in garbage dumps, shantytowns and urban slums. This ministry also helps communities begin and develop farms, gardens and small businesses. As Katherine talked about Impact Ministries, I became intrigued and decided to attend the service. That Sunday, as Steve shared Impact's ministry experiences, my heart burned to encounter the spiritual adventures he was describing. I could hardly contain myself on the drive home after church. I contemplated the different places I could go with Impact Nations and I felt God was highlighting Kenya. I have always wanted to explore Africa, with its diverse cultures, animals and landscapes. As I talked with Doug about going on Impact's next "Journey of Compassion" to Nakuru, Kenya, he agreed it would be a wonderful experience. A month later, Katherine and I met at Starbucks and she thought God was calling her to Africa as well. With Doug's willingness to take care of things at home, Katherine and I began to plan for our trip. My imagination mingled with

God's imagination, and I dreamed of all he had in store for us on this new adventure.

On September 2st, 2013, after much planning and prayer, Katherine and I finally piled our huge suitcases into my jeep and began our long-awaited journey. I felt like God was even more excited about our trip than we were. I sensed he was opening a door so I could see him differently. When I walked through that door, I knew my life would change. Not seeing Zach healed had tainted my perception of God as a healer. I thought the door he was opening might have something to do with healing my small thoughts of him and restoring my hope in the miraculous. Earlier, I had sent an email to Katherine before we left, describing how I imagined our time in Africa would be a runaway train of encounters with God. I shared how I felt like a kid waiting to open the best birthday present ever. As I eyed up my gift, God had playfully told me to wait: "You can shake it and feel it and anticipate it — that is part of the fun, but you need to wait to open it." I had wanted to run and rip off the wrapping paper like a child who cannot delay gratification. Now, God was about to let me rip off the paper, and I felt like a child anticipating Christmas morning.

Doug drove us to Vancouver and took us for lunch at a funky restaurant on Jericho Beach called Galley Patio & Grill, where we gulped down crispy, greasy, outrageously delicious yam fries. Then, we boarded our plane to London, where we would have a layover before flying into Nairobi the following day. Between our excitement over the experiences we were about to encounter and the free glass of wine we received with our dinner, I felt giddy with anticipation. Late the following evening, our plane hit the runway in Nairobi. As Katherine and I were gathering our overhead luggage, a man beside us was texting on his phone and informed a few passengers that there had just been a terrorist attack at one of the malls. As the news settled, we felt somewhat uneasy, but not panicked. Later, we found out Al-Shabab, an Islamic extremist group linked with al-Qaeda, had attacked Westgate Mall. The attack, apparently the worst in Kenya over the past fifteen years, targeted and killed non-Muslims and foreigners. Sadly, members of this terrorist group are still in their youth when they are recruited out of the slums. They are easy targets and will do anything to get out of the abject poverty they face every day.

In spite of the chaos from terrorist threats in Nairobi, Katherine and I had no problem going through customs. As we made our way toward the vans that would transport us to our hotel, there were security guards surrounding the area with AK-47s, but strangely, we were not afraid. God shielded us from fear. By the time we reached our hotel, we were exhausted. We lugged our suitcases up the stairs, eagerly anticipating a warm shower after our ten-hour flight. As soon as we got into our room we opened the door to the bathroom and quickly discovered we would not be having a shower. The faucet limply hung from the ceiling, looking like it was not attached to anything and the shower was only a foot from the toilet. Somewhat disappointed with our primitive bathroom, we climbed into bed, closed our mosquito nets, and slept through the night.

The next morning, the team forfeited going to church in Nairobi due to terrorist threats and made the decision to leave for Nakuru first thing after breakfast. We drove for four hours along a road that paralleled the Rift Valley lowland that extends six thousand kilometres from northern Syria to central Mozambique. The four-hour ride gave us a chance to meet the other fourteen members of our team who had come from Australia, England, Canada, and the United States. Since most of them had been on an Impact trip before, they were able to share stories that stirred up our excitement and our anticipation even more. Before long, we arrived at Hotel City Max in the center of Nakuru, where we would be staying for the duration of our trip.

During our first week in Nakuru, Katherine and I both found that our internal clocks were completely switched around. We would often find ourselves waking up at 2 a.m. ready to take on the day. On one occasion, during the wee hours of the morning, I woke up, showered and got ready for breakfast, thrilled I had finally slept through the night. Puzzled, Katherine asked me what I was doing. "What do you mean?" I asked. "It is one in the morning!" she laughed. Wide-eyed, I went back to bed. On another evening, Steve prayed Katherine would sleep soundly through the night. She did, up until I rudely awakened her, confused yet again by time. I bolted upright in the middle of the night, looked at the alarm clock and realized we had slept in. Katherine was almost impossible to wake up. I shook her three times before she stirred. "Katherine, hurry! We have to get up. We slept in!" Groggily, she looked at the alarm clock, confused. "That is weird," she said. "I didn't hear the Muslim call to prayer. I didn't hear the roosters and I don't hear sounds in the street. Are you sure we slept in?" "Yes! It is a good thing I woke up when I did!" She began to chuckle softly at first and then uproariously. Once again, I was time confused. Night mix-ups continued until we adjusted to the nine-hour time difference.

The first two days in Nakuru were training days, where we gathered in the conference room of Hotel City Max to worship and learn how we would serve during our time in Kenya. Steve taught us how at times God heals instantly, other times incrementally, and sometimes he does not heal at all. Our job is to pray and leave the rest up to God. No matter what happens — whether people are healed or not — they need to leave prayer encounters feeling loved. Steve encouraged us to cross our "chicken lines" and take risks. When we overcome fear and step out of our comfort zones, we can release the power of heaven.

Due to the humanitarian involvement of Impact teams over the years in Nakuru, local dignitaries had honoured the team that had visited in 2012 with a tree planting ceremony. Our team was given the same privilege. We were greeted by government officials and invited to Memorial Park in the center of Nakuru to plant trees, symbolizing how we were rooted in Kenyan soil and a part of their land. What special token of kindness to be able to plant our very own trees! Television, radio, and newspaper crews arrived to film the occasion, and Steve had the opportunity to pray for the nation on public television. Crowds of people began to gather around us, and Steve began sharing about the love of Jesus. Many people that day made a decision to follow Jesus, not through religious manipulation, but through the illumination of Jesus' kindness and hope that he brings to each one of us, especially in our brokenness. Mike Brawan, a local pastor who worked alongside Impact Nations, asked people who responded to Steve's message to share their contact information for further relational connection and practical support. As our team mingled with people and prayed with them about struggles they were having in their lives, I felt fully alive and energized by God's deep concern for the people of Nakuru.

A theme quickly emerging on this journey was the principle of multiplication. Throughout the biblical gospels, there are many stories recorded where people come in droves when they find out Jesus is near. People crowd to see him, bringing their sick friends and relatives. On one occasion, Jesus looks at the crowd numbering more than five thousand people and asks his disciple Philip, "Where shall we buy bread for these people to eat?" (John 6:5) Jesus knows what he is going to do, but he asks Philip to test him. Philip replies that even eight months' wages will not be enough to give each person even one bite of bread. I have to admit, I often relate to Philip, seeing the "not enough" around me and doubting God's ability to provide. Jesus' disciple, Andrew, however, has more faith. He brings forward a young boy who has five small loaves of barley bread and two small fish. Jesus takes this food, looks up to heaven, gives thanks to God, and passes the food to his disciples to be distributed. Everyone present eats as much as they want and there are lots of leftovers! Jesus miraculously multiplies the loaves and fish so there is more than enough. In a similar fashion to this story, God continually moved with the spirit of multiplication amongst our Impact team. He literally took whatever we had and multiplied it as we gave it away. For example, when Pastor Mike went to a store to buy food for one of the slums we were visiting, the storeowner generously quadrupled the amount of food he purchased. Impoverished people in Nakuru were filled with thankfulness as our team gave away medicine, food, love, and hope. At the same time, great joy rose up in our hearts as we witnessed moments of transformation right in front of our eyes. The look of fear in a mother's eyes changed to rejoicing as she realized her child would not die of malaria because we had brought medicine. There are no words to describe the peace I felt about one mother being able to go home assured that her child would live.

We set up our first medical clinic in Mike Brawan's Metro City Church. We noticed that wherever Mike went, darkness would lose its hold. He trusted Jesus to do what he could not do in his own strength. He knew Jesus would provide for the community's needs. His blind faith opened up doors of possibility so God could intervene in powerful ways. Mike's struggles throughout his life had drawn him closer to God so God could transform his heartache into deep wells of compassion. When Mike had been eight years old, his parents had died suddenly and left him orphaned. With no means of surviving, he and his brothers had gone to the local dump and had lived there for four years. He had stolen food and clothing just to survive, and then one day he got caught. His older brother stepped in, shielding Mike from his accusers and telling him to run. Mike had run, but when he had come back later, he found his brother lying on the ground, beaten and dead. Mike rationally had every reason to harden his heart and give up on living a fulfilling, selfless life, yet his pain drove him to make a difference in his community. Today he ministers in the same dump he lived in as a child and he is passionate about rescuing children from lives of hopelessness to give them lives of destiny. He finds them homes and makes sure they have their fees paid so they can go to school. He has helped build over one thousand churches and lives his life by the motto of stopping to help the one. Many of our team's translators were boys Mike rescued off the street, mentored, and helped to establish businesses. I liked Mike's sense of humour and his way of connecting with people in a fun, relaxed and joyful way. He represented hope and love to people who had lost all hope. When I had hard, emotionally draining days out in the slums, I could always count on Mike to lift my spirits.

As people streamed into the Metro City Church clinic, I felt overwhelmed by their needs. The maze of sick people with malaria, dysentery, and infections seemed endless. At this point in my journey, I still tended to look at situations from a limited human perspective, rather than a spiritual perspective as one partnering with Jesus, who could do so much more than my small mind could ever imagine. However, Steve later shared with the team that during the opening prayer over the crowd, a child was cured of a high fever instantly. Other team members began to share their stories. They described deaf ears opening, cataracts disappearing, and blind eyes being restored. A man came in with a cane and left the clinic with it swinging idly in his hand. Each team member had a job, and usually people who were part of the prayer team had the privilege of witnessing these kinds of miracles. The rest of the team had to run the clinic smoothly so mayhem would not break out. I only heard testimonies of miracles that day because my responsibility involved taking people through various stages in the clinic — from intake, to deworming, to the doctor, to the pharmacy. Added to these responsibilities was crowd control. I felt disappointed I had not seen miracles that happened that day first-hand, but I still loved hearing the team's incredible testimonies.

After working in the clinic all day, we left to do an outreach in one of the slums in the evening. We bumped along in the van as we passed wooden market stalls lining the street where vendors sold baskets, jewelry, crafts, fruits and vegetables. The colours of Africa are bright and vibrant. Even in the slums and in the dumps, people dress with brightly coloured scarves, beads, and dresses. In the middle of poverty, colour bursts out, defying the dark, oppressive living conditions. We swerved around rickshaws, bikes, potholes and impatient drivers honking incessantly, to finally reach the slum area. As we pulled in, children came running wildly toward us, laughing and shouting "Mzungu! Mzungu!" This was their word for white person. My heart broke and burst at the same time. I felt waves of pain wash over me as I saw children's appalling living conditions, but these waves mixed with joy at their triumphant spirit and enthusiasm in the face of extreme poverty.

Once again, the beautiful and the ugly collided — children playing, singing, clapping, and rejoicing on one hand, and children with hollow eyes, sniffing solvents to relieve their suffering on the other. Crowded shanties built of plywood, corrugated metal, sheets of plastic, and cardboard boxes lined the dusty road on overcrowded streets. Children ran through the streets barefoot, stepping over sewage and garbage as they rolled tire rims down the streets or played with bits of garbage. I opened up a plastic bag of balloons and went to throw the plastic away, when one of our translators asked, "What are you doing? Don't throw that away! The kids will love to play with it." My heart ached over the gap between this world and mine, while at the same time, I longed to appreciate life's simple gifts as these children were. Steady streams of people gathered around our van to listen and dance to the music being piped out. On the narrow dirt lane, Steve began to share about Jesus, while team members danced and talked with people from the community. When people heard about Jesus' loving kindness, witnessed the joy and hope in the team and community interactions, and experienced profound miracles of healing, their hearts embraced the God who cares for them. Hope was born, as they realized that even if their circumstances did not change, they no longer had to go through life alone as one with no hope.

In their abject poverty, people in the slums could identify with Jesus, who walked this earth with no material possessions of his own. Jesus was poor. All he had he gave away. They were following the one who knew first hand what it was like to suffer. I found many people in Nakuru who had very little giving away what they had, just like Jesus. Sometimes sick people waiting for medicine would let another person go ahead of them in the line to receive medication. Children would split their crayons in half to share with their friends. Children who were hungry and destitute would come along with our team to pray for others in their community. Underneath the ugliness of poverty were the lovely fingerprints of God.

I had to keep reminding myself that God's greater redemptive story can always be mined even during times of crushing darkness. People in Nakuru continually reminded me of this truth. I confess that when I hold my broken dreams in my hands, I still feel some anger toward God. Strong winds of fear still take hold of my heart when I doubt his promises will ever be fulfilled in my life. But in the midst of my fear I realize Zach's story is gaining momentum as the years go on. The ripple effects of love keep going out and will continue to go out, just the same as love keeps going out in those suffering in the slums. With Jesus, nothing is as it seems. He always has a rescue plan. At the time of Jesus' crucifixion it looked like all hope was lost. He was cruelly flogged, mocked and beaten and then nailed to a cross, where he was naked and vulnerable, suffering and dying all alone. But his senseless murder had a redemptive purpose for all of human kind. There is always a greater love story, even within the most heartbreaking stories.

Recently, Alvin, my translator during my time in Kenya, impressed on me how God cares for us during our hard times and gives us the strength to love even when we find ourselves immersed in pain. Alvin taught me how Jesus cares for him in the midst of poverty. Alvin still suffers, but he knows he walks through the heartaches of his life with Jesus. Recently, he sent me an email message sharing how Jesus meets him in the midst of his everyday struggles: "There are so many battles I have to fight, but I am with my amazing God. I have suffered so much and sometimes I have no one to turn to, but I call to God my father and he wipes my tears. He makes me strong." Then, with the heart of Christ, Alvin blesses me even though he has so little: "I have no mother Dana, but since you have shown me love, I feel relieved and happy. I pray God shows you something great when you wake up." What a powerful example of Jesus walking with us through pain so that our love becomes even stronger.

During my time in Kenya, Alvin and I grew close in our few days together. His kindness and goodness blessed those around him wherever he went. He was eighteen years old, close to the age Zach would have been if he were still living. Alvin also had many of Zach's characteristics: a selflessness and depth beyond his years. Most of the other team members had different translators each day, but Alvin and I would search for each other and then spend the day working together. One of the most difficult parts of the whole journey was saying goodbye to him. I wept and wept at the thought of not seeing him again. My mama heart wanted to keep him for myself. Alvin defended the poor and was like a big brother to the children in the slums. They knew they could count on him to check on them weekly. One day, as our team was praying for people, Alvin came over to me and said, "Dana, we have to pray for this little boy. A dog bit his ear and now it is badly infected." We found the boy cowering alone on the side of the road. I placed my hand on his severely infected ear and prayed that God would send his love and healing. To my disappointment, his ear remained the same. I felt angry God had not healed him. If anyone needed a touch from heaven it was this desperate little boy. The random healing I witnessed throughout my time in Kenya confused me. Surely God wanted to heal this broken child. I did not, and never will, understand why God chose not to act on this child's behalf in our moments together. Maybe after we left, God did. I found myself wondering if I was lacking in some way. *Why am I not experiencing healings like the rest of the team? Maybe there is something spiritually wrong with me.* It could be so easy to get sucked into the vortex of discouragement. A sense of betrayal crept in because, once again, I doubted whether God ever heard me. I could not understand why my prayers seemed to go into thin air. I found myself wrestling with my thoughts, confused by God's silence. I felt powerless in my prayers.

On our fourth day in Nakuru, our medical team was given permission to set up a clinic in a Muslim slum called Bondeni, the poorest slum in the city. Never before had a team been given the go-ahead to do this. Given the recent terrorist attacks, our approval was nothing short of a miracle. God had a redemptive plan in his heart for Bondeni and positioned us there at the perfect time. We set up our clinic outside the mosque, spread out on either side of an open sewer. Bondeni has a reputation for being a dangerous slum, so local dignitaries came to ensure we were safe. For the whole day, we did not have a problem. It seemed as though love overpowered any threat of violence. Long hours of working in the clinic sometimes felt overwhelming, but one of the women from the community kindly offered her home to us so we could have a break to eat and get out of the sun. As I made my way to her place, stepping in garbage and debris, I opened the gate into her home and stepped into another world. She had planted colourful flowers along the walkway, and her home was quaint and well kept. In the midst of devastation, she had carved out beauty. An Eden existed in the middle of abject poverty. Her garden represented my life. In the midst of pain and suffering, I too had to make a decision about whether I would make a garden in the midst of the ruins. At first glance, it seemed impossible for beauty to survive within the painful environment of Bondeni, but she made the decision to create loveliness in the midst of desolation. We all have to decide what we will do when we are surrounded with darkness. Will we make room for beauty or will we allow the darkness to invade and take over our lives?

That day, two hundred people received medical care in our clinic, and once again God healed people. He moved compassionately through us, and many Muslims, never having experienced such love, wanted to know about Jesus. A few people from the community shared with our Impact team how they had never seen people love the way we had loved. What they were experiencing was Jesus' love for them, as expressed through our team. I was excited that Jesus healed them as Muslims and then his kindness drew them to his heart. His love is for everyone. His kindness is not exclusively for Christians. No matter where people are at, or what they believe, he takes every opportunity to pour out his love. Jesus does not need a conversion before he shows his compassion to people. Sadly, many Christians approach outreach with a false religious agenda. Conversions become more important than love and I think this grieves Jesus' heart. All Jesus asks us to do is love in his name and he does the rest. In his hands, legalistic religion dissolves. The power of love released heaven in Bondeni.

The following morning, as we were worshipping and praying in our hotel, pastor Mike brought in a woman who needed healing from a bad accident she had been in. We had no idea who she was, but as Steve finished praying for her, tears started streaming down her face, and she smiled, laughed, and cried all at the same time, finally relieved of her chronic pain. Not until the next day did we learn that she was the wife of the UN ambassador from Somalia. She and her husband had come to Kenya because of the recent terrorist attacks. Her husband phoned Mike at six o'clock the next morning, bursting with joy because his wife was completely healed. When Mike asked his permission to share his wife's story, the ambassador said, "Jesus has healed her, and I am happy for anyone to know that." We did not know until later that both the ambassador and his wife are Muslims. Here again, God moved despite differences in belief. The terrorist attacks, although tragic and senseless, had patterns of God's love woven within the tragedy.

One evening, our team planned to go and minister hope to women involved in prostitution. To pay school fees and feed their families, women in poverty are often left with no alternatives. They risk their lives every night so they do not have to watch their children starve to death. We wanted to find these women, love them, and show them a different way. As we piled into the team van at 10 p.m., I felt uneasy and exhilarated at the same time. When you are following Jesus, these feelings often co-exist. When we parked the van, I still felt anxious. The dark, dingy street was not enticing me to go any further. Pushing back against my natural instinct to hide in the van, I joined the group. Gradually, more and more women joined us as we walked down the street until a long line began to form behind us. A police officer, armed with an AK 47 told us to duck into an alley so we would be safe. The police stood watch over us and protected our group. It is so strange how God works. Police officers usually arresting prostitutes now protected them. Almost one hundred women gathered around us, and we began to pray for them. Christina, Steve's wife, shared a story of hope and love. We gave out gift bags, and many women put their names on a sheet to receive follow-up care. Mike would later connect with them and help them get off the streets. The following day, some of these women showed up at Mike's church to receive the spiritual care and practical help they needed.

One of the prostitutes who accepted Jesus' love came into Mike's office with her twelve-year-old daughter whom she had also forced into prostitution to help pay the bills. Weeping, the mother asked Mike to restore her daughter's life. By the next day, Mike had found a way to pay for her school fees so she could get off the streets and go to school. We had the opportunity to meet this young girl, Rose, who now radiated with joy because her life had changed in a moment from despair and hopelessness to joy and hope. I felt the warmth of Jesus' love for Rose and I sensed all of heaven rejoicing in her freedom.

We had an early 4 a.m. start the next morning so we would have enough time to drive for five hours to a remote village inhabited by the Pokot tribe. We grabbed our travel pillows, had a quick bite to eat, and sleepily crawled into the vans. Although we had good intentions of sleeping, we quickly realized the erratic kamikaze driving would keep us more alert than any jolt of espresso. Our drivers insisted on passing each other continuously, driving into Volkswagen-sized potholes that threw us around like rag dolls. The only one sleeping was Steve because he had taken Gravol for carsickness. He flopped around, oblivious to the craziness. After five hours travelling at what felt like the speed of light, we turned onto a steep, dusty dirt road that slowed us down to a snail's pace. The dust billowed into gigantic plumes and, unfortunately, our van was last in line. By now I had figured out the reason for the overzealous passing—nobody wanted to be the poor sucker last in the dusty parade up the mountain. We had women in the front who were too hot, thanks to menopause I am sure, so we had to open up the windows in the back. The dust was so thick in the air, you could have written your name in it.

Our van, obviously the underpowered one of the group, could not keep up with the pace of the convoy and broke down numerous times. Usually a dose of bottled water into the radiator would put some "giddy-up" back into it, and we would be on the road again. On our way up the steep incline to the village, our unreliable ride broke down yet again. We had not seen many people along the way, but as the drivers chatted about how to solve our dilemma, crowds of Pokot people began to form along the side of the road. Steve, in spite of his Gravol issues, enthusiastically jumped out of the van and began talking to them. Soon, they all wanted to know about Jesus. Our new friends wanted a church and, not surprisingly, by the end of the day, Mike had established a relationship with the chief who donated land for a church. This trip was teaching me a lot about moving from the "figure-this-out room" to the "be-fascinated-by-Jesus room."

By the time we finally got to the village, all we could see of one another were layers upon layers of dust on our white shirts and two eyeballs peering out through the brown dust caked all over our faces. We tried to clean ourselves up with sanitary wipes, but it was pointless. We needed a pressure washer! Usually, while travelling to different places in Nakuru, I would purposefully dehydrate myself so I would not have to use the latrines, but this day would be longer than the others, so eventually I conjured up the courage to visit my most feared place. Thankfully, the Pokot latrine was a five-star latrine and had two pieces of cement on either side of the hole so I could step up out of the "who knows what" to do my business.

The people in this tribe knew more than they should have about hunger, disease, and despair. Ravished by drought, the Pokot often lose many of their goats and cattle and can be without food or water for periods of time. Terry Brynan, a nurse who lives long-term with this tribe, brings them medications and clean water, and she educates them about hygiene, worms, disease transmission, malaria, typhoid, and measles. Her tangible help overcomes despair. Through her health care education, she has convinced this tribe to end the controversial practice of female circumcision. Working alongside Terry, we spent the day giving out medications and praying for people. I felt overwhelmed with God's love as his presence swept through this tribe. He poured down his kindness into their lives throughout the day and I felt overjoyed about being a part of what God was doing.

Of all our days in Nakuru, the day we visited the Pokot tribe was my personal highlight. God answered questions that had been lingering in my heart. I had wrestled with God tirelessly about miracles. I grappled with his seeming indifference for some and his instant healing for others. Part of me wanted to push thoughts of miracles into far away places in my mind. It felt too random and unpredictable. I could not bear to look into peoples' disappointed eyes when they were not healed. How could I explain why one person was not healed when another person right beside them was? I had ambivalent feelings, yet a part of me hungered to see healing more than anything. The pendulum swayed back and forth. One minute I was passionate about seeing the supernatural and the next I felt nervous and uncertain. I was so conflicted and tired of thinking about the miraculous that I had asked God not to put me on the prayer team this day, but God had other intentions. I was on the prayer team and God had surprising plans in store for me. The first person I prayed with was healed of blindness. I was shocked and completely not expecting it. God healed even when I had very little faith. In a moment, that woman's life was changed because I had prayed for her. Had I not prayed, she may not have been healed. God and I were working as a team to bring heaven to earth and it felt exhilarating! Apprehension faded away. God's power flowed through me like I had never experienced before. When I placed my hands on deaf ears, people heard. One lady who had her hearing restored started jumping up and down and screaming with delight. For the first time, she heard sounds she had never experienced. God's healing changed peoples' lives in an instant. It was like he was dropping love from heaven. Not only was he healing them, he was healing me. His tangible gifts of love changed my perceptions of him and healed my insecurities that had made me feel like I was spiritually inadequate. I lost track of all the miracles that took place that day. Whatever doubts I had about God using me in a supernatural way vanished. Why God heals some people and not others is still a mystery to me.

Our last clinic was in the Gioto garbage slum on the outskirts of Nakuru. People forage with the pigs for food. There, they rely on trash vans to deliver them with fresh garbage, in which they find their food, clothing, and shelter for the day. My heart could still not fathom the peoples' unshakable spirit and their innate ability to be joyful and loving in such atrocious conditions. One man warmly greeted me and said, "Welcome to our home." I was undone by his humility and hospitality.

Women created beautiful crafts out of plastic garbage bags and recycled paper. Intricately woven garbage bags became colourfully designed purses, and scrap pieces of paper were turned into gorgeous, colourful necklaces. They created beauty out of ashes. Many broken and violent people lived in the dump as well, but in the middle of the darkness, beauty persevered. Jesus, living in the dump with his children, transformed it into a place of hope. When we set up the medical clinic, a health care worker questioned our medical team leader about why we were there and what we were doing. Pastor Mike assured her that we had the authority to be there (which he probably made up on the spot) and then, typical Jesus style, something outrageously good happened. Near the end of the clinic, Mike received a call from a Kenyan government official who was in China. He had heard reports about what Mike and the Impact Team were doing in Nakuru and wanted to voice his appreciation for the work being done for the poor. He then told Mike he was giving him a large, well-stocked clinic so Mike could provide ongoing medical care for people in the community. Again, Jesus lovingly exceeded our expectations.

The one thing that stood out to me most in Kenya was that miracles have many faces. They can look like doctors, nurses, dentists, and volunteers working tirelessly to bring medical care to people in need. They can look like huge smiles in the midst of the worst poverty imaginable. They can look like supernatural healings. They can look like holding little ones close to your heart and giving them human touch they so rarely experience. They can look like sharing tears with a mother who is tired and weary or a mother who has lost a child. Miracles may look different, but the one thing they have in common is this: God's people are bringing heaven to earth.

In some ways, our two weeks in Nakuru felt like a lifetime, and in other ways our time seemed like just a breath. Weary from long working hours, our team piled into a bus that would take us to the airport. As our bus left Nakuru, I was sad to leave the city my heart had grown attached to in such a short time. But I was excited to return to my family and my familiar surroundings. I fantasized about lattes, home cooked meals and the comforts of home. Before going to the airport, Pastor Mike arranged for our team to have lunch at a fancy restaurant in Nairobi. I was dizzy with excitement about ordering a steak and a latte. To my absolute delight and surprise, the barista had created a heart in the foam of my latte. I drank my coffee slowly, appreciating every sip.

Inching our way through traffic, we finally arrived at the airport. The thought of the long journey ahead seemed daunting. It would take eight hours to fly to London, where we would have a long layover before another eight-hour flight to Vancouver. Doug would then pick us up at the airport and drive us the four hours back to Kamloops. As we settled into our seats on the plane, Katherine and I were overcome with fatigue. Our two weeks in Kenya had taken a lot out of us. I could hardly open my eyes to eat. Katherine had reminded me on the way to the airport that I would finally get to have a glass of wine on the plane. I was really looking forward to it, but after ordering it, I could hardly stay awake long enough to drink it. I tried, but my head kept bobbing forward against my will. We slept intermittently all the way to London. Our plan upon arriving in London was to take the subway into the city and visit as many places as we could during our six-hour layover. As soon as we arrived at London Heathrow Airport, we made a beeline to the subway station. Our enthusiasm for our adventure broke all weariness.

Katherine had lived in London from 2004-2005 as a student when she was taking her Master's Degree in International Relations, so she knew every nook and cranny of the city. The sights were magnificent. It was amazing that eight hours of air travel could transport us from the shantytowns of Nakuru to a city filled with cathedrals, art galleries, and castles. The change was refreshing. We stepped from the subway into the pages of a fairy tale. We visited Buckingham Palace, St. Paul's Cathedral, the National Art Gallery, Westminster Abbey, the London Wall, and Trafalgar Square. Every view was breathtaking. London Bridge stretched out across the Thames River, red double decker buses and black taxis lined the streets. We crammed as much as we could into our short time and enjoyed every minute of it. Finally, after seeing all we could, we hopped onto the subway and headed back to the airport. We gave ourselves enough time to enjoy a feast and a cold beer at the airport before we boarded the plane. With plenty of time to spare we ordered our meals and got lost in conversation. We talked about Africa, London and about how we were planning to save the world. When we finally looked at the clock, we realized we had had a bit too much fun talking. Our plane was already boarding and we still had to take a bus to our terminal. We quickly scanned the screens to see where we were supposed to be and then ran. We arrived just as the bus was about to leave to our gate. We laughed nervously at our close call. We did not know how close we had come to missing our plane until some of our team members told us how fervently they had been praying for us because they feared we would miss our flight. We were the last ones on the plane and within moments it left the runway. Once we were settled in and our adrenalin wore off, we slept most of the way back to Vancouver.

When we walked into the Vancouver airport, I inhaled the familiarity of home. It was so good to be back in Canada. Doug greeted Katherine and I with bouquets of roses and I was so glad to see his wonderful face again. I did not realize until that moment how much I had missed him. My exhaustion turned into a manic-type feeling and I could not stop talking for the first hour of our trip back to Kamloops. There was so much to tell Doug and I did not know where to begin, so I just started voicing thoughts in run-on sentences as they came to me faster than I could speak. By the time we got home, I felt like I was going to die of fatigue. Despite my weariness, I was overjoyed to see Lucky and Carter. There is no feeling like being home after a long absence.

One of the beautiful children at our first medical clinic

Katherine and her beloved friend Mark

Precious memories from Africa

The Gioto garbage dump

Bondeni, the poorest slum in Nakuru

Katherine and myself on safari in Nakuru National Park

One of the schools involved in the feeding program

The Lord your God is in your midst—a warrior bringing victory.
He will create calm with his love; he will rejoice over you with singing.

—Zephaniah 3:17 (CEB)

CHAPTER 16

GOD IS LOVE

We should be astonished at the goodness of God, stunned that He should bother to call us by name, our mouths wide open at His love, bewildered that at this very moment we are standing on holy ground.

— Brennan Manning, *The Ragamuffin Gospels*

After coming back from Kenya, I felt compelled to bring the lessons I learned there to my city. God loves Kamloops just as much as he loves Nakuru, and he is eager to be miraculous in our midst even here. Universally, humans are hungry for love, and Canadians are no exception. I often underestimate what a smile, touch, kind word, or prayer can do for someone. Since returning home, my friends and I have gone into the streets of Kamloops with hot coffee on cold days and prayed with people. People often receive these tokens of God's love. Very few people decline prayer. I have to continually overcome my own reluctance to step out and do what I see my Father in heaven doing. He never withholds love. He wants us to join with him and love people back to life.

When I got back from Kenya, I sensed God's love in a fresh, new way. While there, I had seen the eyes of Jesus in those who were suffering. Many people's eyes had held gentleness and kindness despite the pain and suffering they experienced on a day-to-day basis. Their eyes had reminded me of Zach's during his last days with us. They had held hope even during agonizing circumstances. I had seen God's love when people with nothing gave whatever they had to help somebody else. I saw his love in Mark, a special young boy Katherine had met while we were in Nakuru, who had given her a marble and a home-made paper boat as gifts of love, likely the only toys he owned. I had seen God's love when he healed blind eyes, malaria, and deaf ears. I had witnessed heaven coming to earth, even in abject poverty and my heart had changed. It felt warmer and more hopeful in a God who truly cares about what we go through here on earth. Time had allowed me to stand back and gain perspective on how it is possible to live in the tension of the now and the not yet. Not yet are all of God's promises fulfilled, yet I can wait expectantly for them in my life. Now, I still cry daily when I miss Zach so much I can barely breathe. My mind still gets bogged down with unanswered questions that perplex me. God had healed many people in Africa, but there had been many more not healed. I do not understand his ways. He is a mystery.

I still feel confused with God sometimes because he has asked me to endure so much. Yet, because our relationship has weathered many storms, I feel free to be honest about my feelings. When I think of Carter's eyes the morning I told him Zach died, or when I think of watching Zach die little by little, my anger and disappointment with God washes over me as though this tragedy happened yesterday. During these agonizing moments, I cannot justify our pain. No theological explanation of suffering will suffice. For the rest of my life I will battle my loneliness, but I will do so by hoping and trusting in the one who cares about all I go through in this life. God creates resting places for me along the way so I can have a break from pain cycles. Every few weeks, heaviness descends on me and my soul feels like a block of ice. At these times, I struggle to connect with God. I have trouble seeing him, hearing him, or feeling his presence. These times used to make me afraid and panicky. But now, I know God understands me.

During these dry times, I call on my friends and my husband who sustain me with their love until I experience Jesus' love once again. Their prayers bring me back to a tender, personal relationship with Jesus. I believe this life will bring us to the threshold of eternity, where we will see, taste, touch, and hear God's love forever, and never doubt it. But until that time, my journey with God will always have moments of turbulence. Some wounds we are required to carry until we reach heaven, but Jesus never makes us go through life-long wounding alone. He shows us how to walk through painful situations leaning on friends and family, who love and care for us and become physical manifestations of Jesus in our lives.

Forever my joy will always be mixed with sorrow. They are not mutually exclusive. Like paints mixed together, they overlap, and become part of my design and my way of relating to the world. I do not think pure joy exists this side of heaven because there are always bits of sadness woven into my experiences and relationships. At the same time, I look forward in expectation to the day my joy will be pure, never to be stolen from me again. At any moment, our lives may be going well, but in a year, a month, a week, or a moment, trouble will come, guaranteed. The question is what will we do when it does? We have to be anchored in God's love, or we will not be able to handle life's twists and turns. When the bottom drops out, God promises peace because his life and our lives are one. Our family has joined into a story with God that will last forever. Heaven will compensate us for all of our pain. The character George McDonald in C. S. Lewis' *Great Divorce* says, "Heaven, once attained, will work backwards and turn agony into glory."[1] This means every painful experience we have endured on earth will not only be repaired, but somehow things will be indescribably more wonderful because of what we have gone through. I believe that Jesus will give his children a crown when they enter into heaven. The jewels within that crown will be our pain-filled stories that have been turned into glory, forever shining for all of eternity. In J.R.R. Tolkien's *Return Of The King*, the character Sam Gamgee says to Gandalf "Is everything sad going to come untrue?[2] The answer to that question is, undoubtedly, yes. But until that time, God uses people's grief memoirs to bring hope to others as they travel through the valley of sorrows. I have relied on other people's grief journeys to show me the way through pain and their courage has given me the strength to keep going.

Suffering up close looks like a bleeding mess of broken dreams. But from heaven, I have confidence that even our deepest pain stories look like a tapestry of beauty. I believe God stitches together our moments here on earth to form a stunning patchwork quilt, each piece capturing moments of our lives. From our perspective, our quilts can look messy and patternless, like the underside of art. From heaven, however, our life-quilts are beautiful. Even the most heartbreaking pieces of our lives form a design rich with colour and texture, created by the master artist who planned from the beginning how he would turn ugly into beauty. God's compassion fashions loveliness out of all things.

During a recent retreat on Vancouver Island, Katherine and I relaxed under a wooden building called "Wings of Love." Bundled in our winter parkas, we gazed at a stunning view of the night sky, pricked by billions of stars, awed by the greatness of God's glory and love. *Our Milky Way Galaxy is only one out of 170 billion galaxies,* I thought. *The four billion stars shining above us are only a sample of God's greatness.* I was reminded of how big God is compared to anything we come up against during our time on earth. He is bigger than disease, tribulation, and even death. A few shooting stars glided through the inky sky, inviting us to dream big dreams with him. The stars speckling the heavens reminded me of how his mercy and love are infinite. Under his wings of love, I felt excited and optimistic about the future. Hope was ignited. Peace seemed natural. I longed to stay in this place, tucked in his everlasting care. This starry night was one of those special, sacred moments when God's presence was tangible. But I realized faith had taught me how to hold on when I did not feel him near me. Even if tomorrow turned out to be a valley day, I knew I could find refuge under the shadow of his wings. I was confident I could trust him with whatever tomorrow held because he had been faithful during my lowest times. I have learned night seasons are not permanent conditions because I can count on him to rescue me.

The cold winter night's chill was calling Katherine and I indoors. We moved from our quiet resting place and began to walk down the nature trail toward the retreat center. We passed trailheads with names such as "The Path For Hard Times," "The Path of the Waiting Pilgrim," and "The Path of Suffering," and I thought of how each path, no matter how heart wrenching along the way, would have a good ending. I thought back to the names of the radiation rooms in Kelowna that bothered me so much at the time, such as "The Lake," "The Park" and "The Beach." The reason the names troubled me so much was because they did not honour pain and grief. Life is not always about the easy path, and troubled times cannot be trivialized. We need to walk through the hard places we are required to walk through, but we do not have to do it by ourselves. None of us know what pathways we will have to tread, but with Jesus we can be assured each trail eventually leads to eternity where there is no such thing as sorrow and sickness. Before we were born, he knew about the painful places we would travel and he made a way. Through his own suffering, he made it possible for us to find life after death.

You and I have only a short time here on this earth. We are blessed beyond what we deserve, but we are also required to endure much heartache. In the broken moments of our lives, seeds are planted in the very rich soil of God's kindness and when those seeds are showered with his love they bear much fruit and multiply. Just when I thought nothing could grow in the barren waste of broken dreams, seeds began to grow into beautiful plants of love and hope. We are cracked open so that love can be given away. I pray the seeds from our journey are implanted in your heart so that when you walk through the valley of sorrows, you have hope that even the most painful journey can be transformed into a love story.

Under his wings

AFTERWORD

Jesus promises, "on earth [we] will have many trials and sorrows" (John 16:33). He does not mean small glitches in our lives; he means we will have problems that shake us so badly they threaten to snuff us out. I wish our family's story had a nice, tidy ending, but it does not. It will continue to be messy and full of difficult, hard realities, but *when* the storms come, not *if* the storms come, the only place to find refuge is hidden in the rock, Jesus Christ. Covered with his hand, we can endure all things, even death. The raging torrents of heartache can be stilled with one touch of his hand. Throughout our family's journey, I sensed the heart of God breaking for what we were coming up against. In between times of being angry with God, I enjoyed moments when he took me to a quiet place to be refreshed so I could carry on. Not only has the cleft been a quiet resting place for me, but also a place I go to cry out to God so he can defend me. From heaven he hears my cry and comes down to fight on my behalf. The enemy, too strong to fight by myself, now has to deal with God. God is impenetrable in his shield-like protection and completely reliable as a stronghold in times of trouble. When I go into the cleft mourning, God promises me I will come out filled with joy. With bottomless tenderness he says, "My [child], in the clefts of the rock, in the hiding places on the mountainside, show me your face, let me hear your voice; for your voice is sweet and your face is lovely" (Song of Solomon

2:14). During our shared time he does an exchange. He gives me a "crown of beauty instead of ashes", the "oil of joy instead of mourning" and, a "garment of praise instead of a spirit of despair" (Isaiah 61: 3). I come out different than when I went in because the one who loves me infinitely more than I can imagine has held my heart. The one who breathed this earth into being has held me, his child.

Day to day, I must contend with the unhealed parts of my grief. A pain so deep always has new layers to be discovered. I will never be healed, but will always be healing. I need to take trips to the cleft on an ongoing basis so I can be restored. Only one day of forgetting to rest in his arms leaves me lonely, sad and hopeless. A well-worn path finds its way to the cleft, from having travelled there so many times. I rest here and have permission not to figure everything out. I can just put my head on his chest and weep. Words cannot express the myriad of emotions since tragedy descended on my family. Grief still rolls in like a fog and threatens to take me out. But even in these moments I know that through the storm, my king has never left me. Like Lucy in *Prince Caspian,* I shout, "Oh joy! For he is [here]: the huge lion . . . I rush to him. I [feel my] heart will burst if [I lose] a moment ….the next thing [I know is] that I am kissing him and putting [my] arms as far around his neck as [I can], burying [my] face in the beautiful rich silkiness of his mane . . . there must [be] magic in his mane. [I] feel lion strength flowing into [me]."[1] The lion strength of Jesus made it possible for me to step out of the grieving room into a new, bright room where dreams were still possible and life still had meaning. The door between these two rooms swings back and forth so I can move freely between the rooms. I still like to walk into the grieving room and mourn my losses, but I know I am not imprisoned in this room.

My well of joy transcends feelings. I have learned to find joy in all circumstances. Not a giddy joy due to things going my way, but a deeper, wiser joy that comes from knowing I can survive any storm. He already overcame all I would ever face and has said, "It is finished." Before cancer ever hit our family, Jesus had already endured it himself and had provided a path through it for us. For that reason, I can have joy in mourning. Every day my heart grieves and every day I find joy. Jesus touches me so I can press on to the good parts of my life still unfulfilled. He promises to return all that has been stolen from me. I cannot wait to watch Zach grow up in heaven. I have missed watching his life here, and knowing the heart of Jesus, I am convinced I will see the missed years unfold in heaven. I also look forward to seeing Jay with both of his boys again, laughing, playing and rejoicing together for all eternity. Jesus' promises make me want to shout for joy. No matter what we come up against, his "appearing is as sure as the dawn; he will come to us like the showers, like the spring rains that water the earth." (Hosea 6:3) His love never fails.

I am my love's and he is mine,
And this is his desire,
That with his
Beauty I may shine
In radiant attire.
And this will be
— When all of me
Is pruned and
Purged with fire.

— Hannah Hurnard

ACKNOWLEDGMENTS

To Doug, my greatest fan

You expand my heart every day with the grace you have for me and for our family. Without you, I would not be the person I am. You treat me like a princess even when I do not deserve to be treated like one. You serve in big and small ways every day, doing many unglorifying tasks with love in your heart. You are the foundation of our home, drawing out the best in us. Thank you for making *In the Cleft: Joy Comes in the Mourning* a reality, and for supporting me during my despairing moments. You are my best friend.

To Carter, the one who makes my heart come alive

No matter how hard things have been, you are the one who can make me burst into laughter. You are my greatest delight. I can barely believe you are fifteen already. Time has gone much too fast. What you have endured breaks my heart, but I marvel at the strength and compassion you share with others. You have a strong sense of justice, and I love that about you. I can't wait until the day I see you and Zach united in heaven. I miss seeing the two of you together. I am so proud of who you are becoming. Never stop dreaming your dreams. God has breathtaking plans for you.

To Mom and Ray

You have supported me through many storms and through some of the deepest valleys. Thank you for your constant presence and your expansive love. When cancer defined every waking moment of our lives, you were our anchors, securing us when pain threatened to take us under. Your place on Shuswap Lake was a place of respite for us, allowing joy to enter in and massage our bruised hearts. "Grandma and Grandpa's Lake", as Zach and Carter called it, became a place where they could let go of fear and enjoy life's simple gifts: tube rides behind the boat, cliff jumping, swimming and paddling. For a while, they could leave cancer behind and just be kids.

To Dad and Mel

Thank you, Dad, for teaching me how to persevere during tough times. You have taught me to dream big and to live with excellence. When I was a child, you continually taught me to push the envelope and not settle for mediocrity. You also taught me I could overcome anything. Thank you for your influence in my life. Mel, thank you for your encouraging words on my blog that came at the right times.

To Margie, my rock

Thank you for all the tears you have shed with me and for your limitless capacity to love. You were my lifeline when the darkness settled all around me. During my darkest days, you came in, unlatched the window, and allowed the light to flow in. Thank you for your dedication to Zach during his dying. You were my voice when I was too tired to speak anymore. You navigated the medical system when I was confused, and you advocated tirelessly when nobody would listen to me.

To Ryan, who reminds me so much of Zach

Ryan, you have a goal and you go for it. You colour outside of the lines and always move toward your dreams. I love your quiet strength and the way you are with Carter and Ben.

To Darcie, who always moves toward excellence
You inspire me with your big dreams and your refusal to live small. You are the biggest extrovert I have ever met, and your energy spills out wherever you go.

To Kirsten, my warm hearted daughter-in-law
Your kindness fills the room. How you mother Ben delights my heart. I treasure you as my daughter-in-law.

To Benny, my rambunctious, beautiful grandson
You bring life to my heart. Watching you turn into your own little man has been so much fun. You remind me of all that is good in life. You have a brother or sister soon to arrive and I know you will be the best big brother ever.

To Saige, my ever-compassionate niece
I have watched you grow into a beautiful young woman who loves deeply. You are so tender, yet strong and eager to change the world for the better. You work hard and are drawn to excellence. I love being your Auntie.

To Carson, my animated nephew
You make me laugh with your outrageous sense of humour. Whenever I look at you, I see Zach. You and he have the same eyes and it brings my heart joy. Keep pursuing soccer because you are *awesome*!

To Willow and Taylor

You have walked through many storms with us, and nothing is taking us down. We have Laird strength coursing through our veins. I love you both so much.

Grandpa Skye

Life is never dull with you. You never cease to amaze us with your crazy inventions. Zach and Carter loved your "shop" where you indulged them with your imagination and creativity. Thank you for bringing so much joy to them.

Grandma Laird

You have inspired us to live better and more fully. I want to love how you loved. We miss you so much.

Jason Laird

I see so many of your beautiful qualities in our children. Like you, they are tenderhearted, full of love and adventurous. I see your eyes in both of them whenever I look at them. You are forever missed and always close to our hearts.

Katherine Murray

I love our David-Jonathan friendship. I take pleasure in looking at the *Calvin and Hobbes* book you bought me, especially the part when Calvin and Hobbes are racing down the hill on their sled and Calvin says to Hobbes, "If you want to find out where the road goes, get in the fast lane and hit the gas."[1] We are in the fast lane, my friend, just trying to keep up with what Jesus is doing. Thank you for leading me back to the heart of God and for showing me he is all loving and all good. Here is to lattes and adventures of our own. The days will be packed.

Shelley Ockenden

Shell, you became so much more than a nursing support service for us. The first day you met us, you had a hard task before you. Nobody wants to talk to a family about palliative care, but you did it so well. You loved, wept, carried our load, and helped us navigate through the worst season of our lives. I loved you from the moment I met you. Thank you for always remembering to send cards on Zach's birthday and on the anniversary of his death. Thank you for chats over coffee or tea and for being so real.

Dana enjoys hearing from her readers and can be contacted at
danagoodmaninthecleft@gmail.com

About the Author

Dana Goodman's greatest joy in life is Jesus Christ, even on the topsy-turvy days when he is hidden. She loves simple things like hot coffee, deep talks with girlfriends, journaling, spending quality time with her family, mountain biking with her husband Doug, and running with her dog. Her family is her greatest treasure here on earth. She loves to daydream about eternity when she will be reunited with her family. She has a Master's Degree in counselling and enjoys her private practice out of her home in Kamloops, British Columbia.

Dana enjoys hearing from her readers and can be contacted at dana-goodmaninthecleft@gmail.com

END NOTES

Acknowledgments
1. Bill Watterson, *The Days Are Just Packed* (Kansas City: Andrews McMeel Publishing Company, LLC, 1994), p. 19.

Chapter 1 — Who's Who
1. John Muir, *His Life and Letters and other Writings* (Seattle WA: The mountaineers, 1996), p.180.

Chapter 4 — Landmines
1. C. S. Lewis *A Grief Observed* (New York: Seabury, Crossroad, 1961), p18.

Chapter 5 — Tear Soup
1. Nicole Johnson, *Stepping Into the Ring: Fighting For Hope Over Despair* (Nashville Tennessee, 2002), pp. 60–63.

Chapter 7 — Times In Between
1. Anne Morrow Lindbergh, *Gift From the Sea* (New York: Pantheon Books, 1983), p. 18.

Chapter 9 — The Absence Of Light

1. Brennan Manning, *Patched Together* (Colorado Springs: Literary agency Alive Communications, Inc., 2010), Kobo edition.

2. Ann Voskamp, *A Dare To Live Fully Right Where You Are: One Thousand Gifts* (Grand Rapids Michigan: Zondervan, 2010), p. 89.

3. Ann Voskamp, *One Thousand Gifts*, p. 87.

4. Brennan Manning, *The Ragamuffin Gospels* (Colorado Springs, Colorado: Multnomach Books, 2005), Kobo Edition

Chapter 10 — Life In the Valley

1. Anne Morrow Lindbergh, *Gift From the Sea* (New York: Pantheon Books, 1983), p. 91-92.

2. C. S. Lewis, *A Grief Observed*, 24.

3. Ann Voskamp, *One Thousand Gifts Devotional: Reflections On Finding Everyday Grace*, p. 168.

Chapter 11 — Sorrow Unending

1. Don Piper, *90 Minutes In Heaven: A True Story of Life and Death* (Grand Rapids, MI: Revell Publishing, 2004), p. 30–35.

2. Randy Alcorn, *Heaven* (Carol Stream Illinois: Tyndale House Publishers, 2004), p. 472.

3. Brent Curtis and John Eldredge, *The Sacred Romance: Drawing Closer To the Heart of God* (Nashville: Thomas Nelson Publishers, 1997), p. 154.

Chapter 12 — Lamentation

1. Nicholas Wolterstorff, *Lament For A Son* (Grand Rapids Richigan: William B. Eerdmans Publishing Company, 1987), p. 6.

2. Nicholas Wolterstorff, *Lament For A Son*, p. 57.

3. Gerald Sittser, *A Grace Disguised:* How the Soul Grows Through Loss (Grand Rapids Michigan: Zondervan Publishing House, 1996), p. 19.

4. Nicholas Wolterstorff, *Lament For A Son*, p. 35.

5. C. S. Lewis, *The Problem of Pain* (New York: Macmillan Company, 1962), p. 93.

6. Brennan Manning, *Patched Together*, Kobo Edition.

Chapter 13 — Aftermath

1. C. Baxter Kruger, *The Shack Revisited* (New York: Faith Works, 2012), p. 6.

Chapter 14 — Beautiful Things Out Of Dust

1. Gerald Sittser, *A Grace Disguised: How a Soul Grows Through Loss* (Grand Rapids Michigan: Zondervan publishing House, 1996), p. 104.

2. Eden and Brad Jersak, *Rivers From Eden: Forty Days of Intimate Conversations With God* (Abbotsford BC: Fresh Wind Press, 2004).

3. C.S. Lewis, *A Grief Observed*, 58.

Chapter 15—Nakuru, Kenya

    1. Impact Nations, http//www.impactnations.com, (January 16, 2014).

Chapter 16—God Is Love

    1. C. S. Lewis, *The Great Divorce* (New York: Harper One, 1946), p. 69.

    2. J.R.R. Tolkien, *The Lord Of The Rings: The Return Of The King* (Houghton Mifflin Publishing Company, 2003), p. 246.

Afterword

    1. C. S. Lewis, *Prince Caspian* (New York: Harper Trophy, 2000), p. 141–143.

CPSIA information can be obtained at www.ICGtesting.com
Printed in the USA
BVOW08s2007050914

365564BV00004B/11/P

9 781498 408